"Time in a Bottle *is a must-read for all who desire a life filled with love, satisfaction, and success. Integrating spiritual principles with quantum physics in an easy-to-understand way, Howard Falco pulls back life's curtains and shines a bright light on what it takes to co-create the life of your dreams."*
—**Arielle Ford,** author of *The Soulmate Secret* and *Wabi Sabi Love*

"In this inspiring book, self-empowerment expert Howard Falco provides insights and ideas that show you how to fulfill your deepest desires by mastering the way you think about and use your time. If you are ready to reach your goals and achieve greater happiness, make time to read Time in a Bottle!*"*
—**Amanda Owen,** author of *The Power of Receiving* and *Born to Receive*

"A must-read that transforms the reader from victim to victorious. An empowering spiritual guide that, from the inside out, helps the reader to master life."
—**Susan Stackpole,** host of the radio show *YOUnique! Life Starring You*

"This outstanding book is a significant achievement in spiritual technology, marrying broad-stroke metaphysical truth with practical grounded examples and techniques for healing and transformation."
—**Dr. Darren R. Weissman,** developer of the LifeLine Technique and author of *The Power of Infinite Love & Gratitude*

"This is a must-read book for anyone looking to live life out loud— inspired and motivated to passionately and purposefully live life as it is meant to be lived, consciously, creatively, and powerfully!"
—**The Reverend Dr. Raymont Anderson,** life coach, minister, author of *Moving Mountains,* and regular contributor to Examiner.com

"With a remarkable ability to make complex subject matter comprehensible, Howard Falco explains how your beliefs, thoughts, and feelings create your experience of time."
—**Jarl Forsman** and **Steve Sekhon,** authors of *Wise, Happy and Feeling Good*

TIME
in a
BOTTLE

TIME
in a
BOTTLE

MASTERING THE
EXPERIENCE OF LIFE

HOWARD FALCO

JEREMY P. TARCHER/PENGUIN
a member of Penguin Group (USA)
New York

JEREMY P. TARCHER/PENGUIN
Published by the Penguin Group
Penguin Group (USA) LLC
375 Hudson Street
New York, New York 10014

USA · Canada · UK · Ireland · Australia
New Zealand · India · South Africa · China

penguin.com
A Penguin Random House Company

Most Tarcher/Penguin books are available at special quantity discounts for
bulk purchase for sales promotions, premiums, fund-raising, and educational
needs. Special books or book excerpts also can be created to fit specific needs.
For details, write: Special.Markets@us.penguingroup.com.

Library of Congress Cataloging-in-Publication Data

Falco, Howard.
Time in a bottle : mastering the experience of life / Howard Falco.
p.   cm.
ISBN 978-0-399-16188-9 (pbk.)
1. Self-realization.   2. Time—Philosophy.   3. Time management—Philosophy.
4. Conduct of life.   I. Title.
BF637.S4F353   2014   2013050135
158—dc23

Printed in the United States of America
1   3   5   7   9   10   8   6   4   2

Book design by Meighan Cavanaugh

Within you is the creative power of the universe.
Avoid this truth and stay victim to time and circumstance.
Embrace this truth and time and circumstance
will endlessly be determined by you.

To Humanity: Master Thyself

CONTENTS

PART IV. TRANSCENDING TIME

(Discovering Eternal Joy)

Introduction

ETERNITY IS JUST A MOMENT AWAY

Of all the resources in the universe, the one that is more valuable and highly coveted than any other is the resource of time. It is more precious than gold, more desired than money, and more needed than love. It is the single most important aspect of life. The simple truth is that without time, nothing else matters.

Our misunderstanding of time—how our thoughts relate to time, how time is actually created, and how time seems limited— is one of the biggest reasons we suffer and at times feel hopeless or powerless in our lives. It is one of the main reasons we don't act on our dreams or actually work to fulfill our deepest desires. The result is unanswered questions and a life that tends to feel unfulfilled. It may be "time" for the idea of time to change.

What if you understood the power of time so well and to such a deep level that you could transcend the way these limiting beliefs restrict you and keep you from what you intend to create for yourself? What if you could learn how to consistently put time on your side? *Time in a Bottle* is a book about doing just that. It is about mastering the creative process of life by mastering the concept of time.

> "Being rich is having money; being wealthy is having time."
>
> —MARGARET BONANNO

The best way to liberate yourself from time and thus more deeply understand it is to work to discover the limiting beliefs that keep you from creating what you want out of life. To gain a greater awareness of why these deeply held beliefs have existed. The next step is to question whether or not these limits are really true, maybe for the very first time. The final step is to sincerely reflect on whether these long-held ideas about yourself and your world serve you and your creative desires and intentions from *this moment forward*. There is great transformative power in this process. A new way of seeing and experiencing the world awaits you.

ON MY PERSONAL PATH of awakening to the great power we each possess within ourselves, one of the most astonishing realizations I came to is about how the experience of time is created and how powerful an impact it has on the way each of our lives unfolds. It is a new way of looking at time that changes everything. A mastery over the concept directly relates to a sense of personal fulfillment and mastery over life itself.

. . .

MY JOURNEY to these understandings started in 2002, when, at the age of thirty-five, my life took an astonishing turn. Happily married with two children and a successful career, I had simply reached a point in my journey where I was questioning everything about the nature of my existence and my purpose in the world. I was questioning the very reason for life itself. I had a great family, good friends, and a job that was providing a decent living. Yet I had an unsettled, nagging feeling inside of me. A deeper meaning, understanding, or connection to life seemed to be missing. The hardest part of all of this was the fact that there wasn't anything that I could pinpoint that was wrong. In fact it was just the opposite. On the surface everything seemed right.

Many people often attribute unhappiness to specific unfulfilled desires: "I haven't found the right soul mate, the right career, my true passion, or the health and vitality I've always wanted." I didn't have any of these issues at the time, which made my restlessness much harder to accept. This was a very unsettling place of mind to be in. There had to be a reason for the gnawing discontent. Something was pushing me to know more. There had to be answers to the larger questions I had about some of the biggest mysteries of life. Either way, I had come to a place where I didn't just desire to know the answers to my deep questions any longer; I *yearned deeply* for this insight. My heart ached for this wisdom.

Over the course of the next four months, the miraculous occurred as my readiness and deep desire were met by this elegant universe in an explosive expansion of awareness and understanding about the nature of existence that to this day is still beyond what can be expressed in words. Overwhelming, knee-bending humility pervaded me as this new understanding took hold. This was immediately followed by a sense of complete unworthiness to be experiencing the breadth of this vast ocean of universal wisdom. So strong was this feeling that it took me more than two years to fully accept that this expansion in consciousness had actually happened to me and to embrace the fact that I, like every other person in the world, am worthy of this grace and all that it offers.

How did this happen to me? The buildup to it seemed to involve some combination of my long-held questions and deep curiosity about life, the inability to find peace with my daily experience, and a real readiness to truly admit, "I don't have the answers—I don't know." This curiosity and readiness put me in such a receptive state of mind that I was more open to receive new information than I ever had been in my entire life. I did not care how the information would change me—I was open to it at any cost. As my awakening began I suddenly realized that the information I was looking for over many years was already present within the everyday happenings and details of my daily existence, minute by minute, hour by hour, and day by day. The answers had always been right in front of me!

In a flash, an instant, the true purpose of life revealed itself to me: the continuing expansion of my understanding and awareness about the nature of who I AM. All human behavior, action and reaction, joy and suffering, the beauty and divinity of all things— it all made sense all at once. Where before I saw the whole puzzle of life from a place inside the puzzle where it was difficult, if not impossible, to see how one piece connected to another, I now looked down upon the whole picture where each piece and its connection to every other became crystal clear.

The meaning, perfection, and synchronicity of every single particle of matter were revealed. The purpose of each event of life became self-evident. A new understanding emerged that exposed how all the happenings in my experience were connected to my journey. For the very first time I understood that the great power to create and shape the content and the context of the experience of life was within each one of us, just waiting to be discovered.

In an effort to honor this grace and the incredible insight into the nature of self-awareness that I had been granted, I wrote my first book, *I AM: The Power of Discovering Who You Really Are*, which was published in 2010. In my travels over the past four years, and in my one-on-one work with hundreds of people, the biggest question I am asked is "How?"—"How can I make the changes I want in my life? How can I overcome the circumstances that are holding me back? How can I realize my dreams?" The most empowering answer to every single one of these questions stems from a new understanding of *time*. This is the cornerstone to a new understanding of life.

THIS BOOK'S MAIN INTENTION IS to guide you through an in-depth look at the core mechanics behind the way your true thoughts and desires turn into your experiential reality. Whether it is the desire for career or financial success, a more meaningful relationship, or just more peace of mind and clarity in your daily journey, *Time in a Bottle* not only explains exactly how these new intentions are actually created but also how the idea of time plays a key role in the process. As you'll learn throughout the pages of this book, the power to determine time and how it influences the unfolding of your life is always in your hands.

What could be more liberating than coming to the realization that you have a choice in every moment and in every circumstance? What could be more empowering than knowing that you are always in control of time?

You will learn the tools of the mind, and even more important, gain the insight required to create or collapse time as it relates to love, money, career, health, and any other personal desire.

The book is broken down into four unique parts. Part I takes a look at the overall big picture regarding the purpose of time as it relates to life. The concept of infinity is presented, along with the reasons why understanding this concept is necessary for you to experience a more liberating state of mind. The way you connect to life and how important this connection is to the creative process are explained in detail, along with the exact purpose of all of your challenges along your travels. This grander and deeper view of the cosmology of life is a very important foundation for those looking for the most empowering understanding of the way time works for you or seems to work against you.

Part II discusses the beliefs, thoughts, feelings, and actions that actually produce the force that creates "time" and keeps what you desire away from you longer than you'd like. This critical understanding reveals the keys to creating the best state of mind possible to get on with the business of moving you closer to everything you want.

Part III is about the awareness needed to fuel your ability to create. This section helps make the process of manifesting very clear for you. It is about learning how creating what you want can be something that flows as naturally as possible, rather than being something that feels like work or something that needs to be forced. Part III presents a way of creating that simply and beautifully reflects a new version of who you are or who you are becoming. It's about immersing yourself by way of a new awareness into the very empowering, timeless, and creative moment that is now.

Part IV builds on all the previous sections in an effort to transcend the negative aspect of time completely. It is about bringing you to a way of being in the world where every moment of life is embraced for its purpose and value. Here you are taken to a state of mind where a deeper recognition of the elegant nature of life provides for the most powerful concept of them all to be embraced and demonstrated: faith. This is not a faith that asks you to merely accept what you are told, or a faith that requires no participation, but rather a faith that works from a deeper understanding of the perfection of not only your own life but of all the other endless expressions of matter around you. Embracing this understanding is the last ingredient in the elixir that allows you to be a master of your reality.

When I look back on the unfolding of my own life, I am struck by the undeniable precision with which everything has happened. From the bigger challenges and heartbreaks to the greater joys and successes, each event has been linked with synchronicity to a greater intention that I have deeply pursued in the world. Each painful lesson, emotion, or feeling that things were taking too much time was necessary, even down to the most finite detail of the experience. Whether I understood these challenges at the moment they were happening matters not, because what I am certain of now is that every single one of these life lessons played a vital role in what unfolded next along each moment of my particular journey.

It seems like just yesterday that I looked at people I met, passed on the street, or knew in some fashion as though they seemed to have everything I wanted to create. I wondered to myself, "How in the world did this happen for them? How did they find their soul mate, their dream job, a peaceful and confident state of mind?" Or, even more important, "How in the world is this going to happen for me?" Many of my dreams and goals seemed so far away and so unreachable that when I was younger it was often too painful to even think about.

There is an old saying, "Where there is a will there is a way." This goes straight to the heart of where the power of creation gets its extremely potent nudge. When I look at my past goals and desires, I am astonished at how many that I had dreamed about, envisioned, or written down actually have materialized. This is a testament to life and how it is here to work with you and the intentions you hold in your mind. It is here to help you every step along the way.

Every dream and idea we focus on has a particular set of conditions that need to come together for that specific intention to be realized. This sets the timetable for each intention on the journey to its realization. What *Time in a Bottle* presents is the awareness of how much your deepest truths, thoughts, feelings, and actions affect how fast these vital conditions come together that make your deepest wants and desires a reality.

An analogy would be to think of time from the perspective of using a magnifying glass to start a fire. A magnifying glass takes the light and energy from the sun, and through the curvature of the glass, concentrates that energy on one small spot of kindling, producing a high level of heat. This concentration of heat is what is needed in order to ignite the kindling. The longer it takes to focus the energy on one spot, the longer it will take to start a fire.

Your intentions are just like this. You have to have enough willpower to focus on your intentions long enough, with the right amount of precision on what you want and how to accomplish it, for your intended reality to ignite. The process of putting together the right conditions to harness the energy of creation in your favor—to achieve your intentions and desires—is what this book is dedicated to offering.

Time in a Bottle also deals with many of the challenges we each face in life and shows how a deeper understanding of time grants us the strength and fortitude needed to overcome any perceived obstacle or setback we encounter.

For example, a tough economy or work environment may cause some to look for answers as it relates to improving their finances or finding a job. Or, relationship issues could have some constantly asking why it takes so long to find the right one. The book will show that the mind-set you adopt in the face of any of these challenges is directly related to the *time* it will take to get through to the desired result. Your way of looking at a particular situation can spark creativity and collapse time, or it can inhibit creativity and stretch time. How this mind-set has been formed and how to change it will be specifically addressed.

"Time is really the only capital that any human being has, and the only thing he can't afford to lose."

—THOMAS EDISON

ONE WHO MASTERS THE CONCEPT of time is one who masters the concept of life, as intention, state of mind, and choice synchronize. Many throughout the world have demonstrated this over and over again through their creative endeavors. Whether it is the man or woman who survives the sudden loss of a loved one and then finds the strength to go out and start a new, joyful, and loving relationship, or whether it is the person who suddenly loses his or her job and immediately finds a way to create a much more fulfilling vocation, the approach is the same. We have seen this in President Barack Obama's incredibly quick rise to becoming president and in Steve Jobs's lightning-fast development of successful, new products during his second reign at Apple. What is always on display in life is how intention, belief, awareness, and action come together to create results that seem to defy any preconceived logic of time.

Holding limited ideas about time, or fearing that one lacks enough of this endless commodity, is what leads to a feeling of constant pressure in one's life. Ironically, this constant pressure ages the mind and body at an accelerated pace and wears down one's soul and spirit. The ability to master time, however, is available to anyone who has the true will and desire to understand the essence of the process. The result is a priceless freedom of mind and a powerful release of previously untapped raw creative energy.

To live timelessly, peacefully, and powerfully, one must learn to be in what has been called the *Zen*, the *present* moment or the *flow* of life. Therefore, the main crux of this book will be to explain how to arrive at this seemingly elusive state of mind. Each moment of consciousness and how it is textured and colored are always based on the truest thoughts and beliefs of the observer. This observer is always you. **These thoughts determine whether you are contributing to the state of mind that quickens the pace of creation for what you desire to be true, or whether you are expanding the amount of time it takes to experience these desires.** Either way, the dominant presiding factor comes from within you. It emanates from your will to become more conscious about the way you see yourself and your world. It is this continuous perception-reaction cycle that determines the quality of energy you emit on a daily basis. This energy affects everyone and everything around you, and it determines exactly how life responds back to you.

Time in a Bottle is dedicated to enlightening you to the great creative power you have within yourself to determine "time" and how to best manage it as you journey to a greater awareness and realization of your deepest dreams and desires. May your creative experience in this lifetime be more peaceful and full of love because of this.

"All of my possessions for a moment of time."

—QUEEN ELIZABETH I

The Holy Grail

Elusive throughout the ages
Searched for over the centuries of time
Humanity has been unable to produce it
Not one has been able to find
This cup that holds such promise
Of powers beyond compare
The confused crave its magic
The fearful don't even dare
Blind are all these seekers
Who believe it's a possession to crave
This grail belongs to every person
Graced from birth to grave
The cup is the source of wisdom and strength
Mistakenly sought over the ends of the earth
Those who come to its understanding
Will experience eternal rebirth
This treasure is with you always
Never lost so you cannot find
One day realizing it couldn't be closer
For the Holy Grail is the power of your mind.

PART I

THE PURPOSE OF TIME

(Why Life Is)

"Time is what keeps everything from happening at once."

—Ray Cummings

ACCEPTING INFINITY

Every piece of data-collecting technology that mankind has ever used to study the stars and the heavens has consistently led us to the unavoidable conclusion that the universe is without end. We have yet to bump into a wall or boundary that marks a spot somewhere out in the vastness of space that says "this is where reality stops." So far, our astronomers have discovered no *Truman Show* moment. In fact, the more high powered the technology we develop to look deeper out into space, the farther space seems to go. The result is that the more our curiosity drives us to look "beyond," the more we discover there is to explore. There seems to be quite a message coming to us in this particular endless conundrum. Might there be a better place for us to spend our time looking for answers? As we exhaust ourselves in the ironic outer search for *insight* and understanding, the whisper to *"look within"* seems to get louder and louder.

What astronomers and cosmologists do continually discover in their ongoing search is an endless ocean of more than 300 sextillion stars (a sextillion is 1,000 trillion), at last published estimated count. There seems to be an endless stream of stars and galaxies in all stages of the birth and death cycle in the universe. Some of these are nebulas of stars just being born; others are older stars exploding or collapsing in on themselves and dying. The overwhelming point is that the process of creation, or what is called the universe, stretches as far as the eye, with all its magnifying technology, can see. One can only faintly imagine how many stars and galaxies might be beyond the limits of our current awareness. The contemplation of such expansiveness can boggle the mind.

ONE OF THE MOST LOGICAL conclusions to draw from the scientific data we have is the notion, concept, or just plain reality of **infinity. The universe is without end.** From this self-evident truth the next logical conclusion one could draw is that a universe that is without end must also be without beginning. Not finite, but infinite. This is the point where the mind is likely to say, "Huh?" The idea of something with no beginning and no end can seem more than a bit overwhelming to the human psyche. The reason for this is that we are very much conditioned by everything we experience on a daily basis. We look for and actually crave structure in order to survive. Everything we experience in the material world has a beginning and an end, boundaries. From human beings, animals, and plants, to mountains, planets, stars, and galaxies, everything in existence emerges from a formless unbounded wave of energy and potential into some *thing*, some form or shape or being, and then takes the journey dissolving itself back into nothing again. Thus the endless cycle of birth and death surrounds us. During this journey, it is our boundaries that give us distinction and allow us to experience our existence. Our boundaries give us life.

To think of something that is not subject to the limits of beginning and end can be a tall order for the mind to grasp. On the road to mastering time and its influence on your life, however, it is vital that you begin to stretch your awareness to grasp the nature of infinity and its role in your life. An expansion of awareness, especially as it relates to this very large concept, is directly related to an increase in your ability to consciously create what you desire. The process of contemplating and realizing the truth of infinity has the powerful effect of reducing fear in your life. **Eliminating or overcoming many of your fears will enable you to freely walk through the doorway to the greatest personal and spiritual liberation possible.**

DEMONSTRATING INFINITY

Webster's dictionary describes infinity as the unlimited extent of time, space, or quantity. This is exactly what the universe is showing us each time we take a deep look. One look up at the endless number of stars in the sky on a crystal-clear night can stir a sense of wonder at this mystifying vastness. When contemplating this concept, we can begin to see the absolute perfection of the process of life as it relates to infinity. These thoughts can bewilder the mind. The definition of infinity can be so simple in one way and so mind-blowing in another. Looking at the big picture, however, provides a necessary foundation for a new mindset and more of the practical day-to-day creative information that is yet to come in this book. Understanding this concept is a huge key to unleashing your creative power, so please do not hesitate to read this over again and again as necessary. Here we go . . .

Infinity is *everything*. Since everything in this definition includes both what is manifest (exists in the known universe) and un-manifest (all possibilities yet to exist), it is all possibility at once. In order for infinity to be *realized*, or known as true, all possibilities must be demonstrated. The demonstration of all possibility at once would lead to no individual thing (no-thing) but all things simultaneously, or what is commonly called "oneness." Oneness cannot be realized, however, because there would be no way, no one, or no-thing to observe or experience it. Oneness would actually be the dissolution of space and time, because at oneness, space and time would no longer be necessary. The never-ending experience of space and time, however, is necessary as the pathway for infinity to be true. For infinity to be true or "validated," all possibility must be true *without end*. **Therefore, there is no end to creativity. There is no end to life. There is no beginning or end to time.**

What is so incredibly elegant about the experience of life is the way that this great truth is demonstrated. It is demonstrated through the experience of space and time, or what is called *reality*. Life is the process through which infinity is demonstrating itself. **"I AM that I AM." Life is the never-ending journey of the "experience" of the manifestation of all possibility from every perspective.** This moment and your observation of it is simply one of an infinite number of perspectives and possibilities that exist. Each one is vital to the experience of infinity in the whole unending universe.

Is this deep enough for you? Again, this fundamental understanding of the grander view of life is critical at this beginning stage of the book and a very important foundation for the more practical information yet to come regarding how much you matter and how you are influencing time. It is this foundation that ultimately reveals how powerful you are and what an incredible endless influence you have on so much of the creation of your reality!

What TIME does is allow the SPACE for possibility to manifest. This is also known as EVOLUTION. Life and its infinite possibilities emerge and are realized through the context of time and space. Time produces space. Space combined with time makes room for individual possibilities to evolve. Your observation of creation and your demonstration of the unending stream of newly learned possibility for yourself is what life and the expression of infinity are all about.

An analogy that might help demonstrate this is that of a fulllength movie reel. Let's say the full-length reel represents all possibility or oneness (some have expressed this as "singularity"). A tightly wound reel of film by itself titled "Life," however, does not convey the real meaning or experience of the movie. The reel has to be played out frame by frame so that you can experience each scene and each word in order to get the full experience of the movie and "know" its true meaning. This is exactly what "time" provides for you. It allows you to experience each frame of your life right in front of your eyes, moment by moment, at a pace that is determined by you. It also leads you to a more and more powerful understanding of the real oneness of all of life.

Here is where it gets even more interesting and extremely exciting. Not only do you decide the pace of time as it relates to many of your creative expressions, but you are also the director, writer, and producer—you decide the story, content, location, and characters. **What is even more exhilarating and empowering is that right now, as the writer, you have the opportunity to change the story and its context in any single moment.**

Life is a continuous stream of experience. By allowing yourself to open up to new ideas and thoughts, you are giving yourself a greater understanding of what your journey is all about. This expanded awareness is what allows you to make clearer and stronger choices for your life. This is how your life evolves day to day, week to week. Your journey of evolution is a result of the new self-defining choices that have resulted from this expanded awareness.

In my first book, *I AM: The Power of Discovering Who You Really Are*, I explain the process of personal evolution.

Evolution is creation expressed. Creation and evolution are both happening in every moment. The main distinction is that creation is the process and evolution is the term given to the measure of the process. The stage to observe this process is where relativity and time come in. Relativity makes the distinction of all things possible and time allows for it to unfold in a way that is observable and experiential.

EINSTEIN'S DISCOVERY OF THE SIMPLE and elegant equation $E=MC^2$ as the special theory of relativity gives us a window into the creation of matter and the relationship between you and time. What is most interesting about Einstein's equation is the squaring of the speed of light. Einstein realized that "time" is not the constant in life. He realized that time is relative to the observer—you! The constant in the equation is always the speed of light because Einstein concluded that nothing can catch the speed of light. As soon as any object were to travel fast enough to begin to approach the speed of light the universe would make adjustments, transferring energy into the mass of the object in order to slow time and protect the ratio of the speed of light to the object, thereby keeping it constant. The result is that no object can get in front of light. The mass of the object, the experience of time, and energy all change in order to keep the speed of light constant at 186,282 miles per second.

This single truth provides the groundwork for some very interesting ways of looking at reality and exactly how you create for yourself. One of the only other things I can think of that one can never seem to catch, measure, or get in front of is a thought. Since all thought stems from an intention, we can make a very interesting connection between intention, the speed of light, and Einstein's equation.

What if instead of using the speed of light squared (C^2) in the equation, we replace C^2 with I for Intention? This is how the equation would look:

E (Energy) = M (Mass) × I (Intention)

WHAT IS INTERESTING about looking at the equation this way is how it relates to a modern concept of quantum physics. In this field of study, physicists have discovered, by looking deep into the atoms of matter, that what is being observed acts either like a wave of energy (pure, formless potential) or a particle (a piece of solid matter), depending on the presence of an observer. In other words, matter is only detectable when there is someone paying attention; otherwise, it remains as a wave of pure potential. *Attention*, which stems from *intention*, seems to be the critical determining factor that leads to how matter is held together. The observer and creator is always you!

This single idea is the absolute validation of how much you matter. You are integral to everything you come in contact with, everything you direct your attention on, and every choice and action you take in the world. You have a massive influence and significance in every aspect of your life!

In the famous "double slit experiment," which turned the science world on its head, this was proven to be true. In this experiment, scientists shot electrons (extremely tiny pieces of matter) through two slits, and measured their projection pattern on a screen against the wall. The scientists thought they would end up seeing two lines on the screen that corresponded to the two slits that the electrons passed through. Instead, what they saw was an interference pattern across the screen. The interference pattern indicated that the electrons did not act like individual pieces of matter as they went through the slits, but rather, the electrons acted like a wave of potential. Even when the scientists shot the electrons through the slits one at a time, the same interference pattern emerged! This indicated that each electron started as a particle and turned into a wave of pure potential. As a wave of possibility the electrons exhibited all possibilities at once going through both slits as a wave and colliding or interfering with itself on the other side, thus producing the interference pattern on the screen. What scientists had thought was matter in the smallest detectable form turned out not to be solid, but to exhibit itself as both a particle at times and a wave of all possibilities.

To get more data on this unique and puzzling finding, physicists decided to put a measuring device near the slits to see how the electron managed to change from a single piece of matter into a wave as it passed through the slits. What happened next is what really baffled them. When the measuring device was in place, and they again shot the electrons through the slits, the electrons went back to behaving like particles (matter), producing just the two lines on the screen against the wall. No interference pattern was discovered. The pattern changed because the electrons acted as solid matter, as though they knew that they were actually being watched, measured, and observed.

"As a man who has devoted his whole life to the most clear-headed science, to the study of matter, I can tell you as a result of my research about atoms this much: There is no matter as such. All matter originates and exists only by virtue of a force which brings the particle of an atom to vibration and holds this most minute solar system of the atom together. We must assume behind this force the existence of a conscious and intelligent mind. This mind is the matrix of all matter."

—MAX PLANCK (THEORETICAL PHYSICIST
WHO ORIGINATED QUANTUM THEORY)

AT THE MOST FUNDAMENTAL LEVEL of matter, it has been revealed that the observer (you) is who is having the greatest impact on how reality expresses itself. You are the key in the equation. What holds all matter together is the observer, an awareness or "consciousness."

Rearranging Einstein's equation makes this even clearer (again using Intention to replace the speed of light squared).

E (Energy) = M (Mass) x I (Intention)

or

$$\frac{\text{E (Energy)}}{\text{I (Intention)}} = \text{M (Mass)}$$

$$\frac{\text{E}}{\text{I}} = \text{M}$$

This is the general formula for creation. Creation is the continual process whereby pure, formless

**Energy (E) is continually divided by
Intention (I) and formed into Matter (M).**

**Thought creates reality.
Mind becomes matter.
I must become AM.**

THE WAY YOU CHOOSE TO see yourself as an individual "I" is destined for the experience of "AM" as your intention takes your energy and turns it into matter in an infinite number of ways. The energy of the whole universe is divided and rearranged by all creative intention (thought), or what is known as the collective consciousness. This intention is the driving force of the whole equation!

As Niels Bohr, the Danish physicist who made significant

foundational contributions to the understanding of atomic structure and quantum theory, once stated, **"Anyone who is not shocked
by quantum theory has not understood it."**

So the purpose of time is to give life the space to unfold and
demonstrate its glorious infinity. Think of all of the endless creative expressions that have unfolded on our planet over millions
and millions of years. Since the cooling of the Earth there has
been a continuous process of transformation all across the globe.
These changes take shape through volcanoes, ice ages, earthquakes, and floods, forming all of the planet's thousands and
thousands of rivers, lakes, and oceans. Millions of species of plants
and animals have evolved. Since mankind entered the picture, the
creative manipulation of matter has been taken to a whole new
level of complexity.

We have gone from using sticks and rocks as tools to accomplish
what we need to survive to using industrial machinery, technology,
and computers where high-speed bits of data travel wirelessly from
one end of the world to the other in fractions of a second. Time is
what allows all of these creative expressions and all other possibilities yet to manifest to unfold and to be experienced.

The constant process of birth and death that you witness all
around you is the evidence of the inability of matter to remain as
one individual thing (some-thing). It must prove itself to be part
of everything or no individual thing (no-thing) by recycling itself
back into the very essence from which it came. At the same time
it must prove itself to be some-thing again: I AM.

The transformation of matter can be compared to the journey

water takes through the process of condensation and evaporation. Water rises and evaporates, turning into vapor or mist, only to condense again into a liquid as it cycles through this endless process. From a seemingly formless body of water to a single drop that literally vaporizes—this is a metaphor for the journey of everything in existence. From the acorn that grows to be a mighty oak and eventually dies and turns into mulch, to the wrinkling of your skin and the aging of your body back to dust: The endless journey of energy into matter is at the heart of the process of life. Death is the process of rebirth; infinity simply is.

Along this never-ending journey of energy to matter you are shaping it and having a very direct effect on it in some way. That is how powerful you are and how important you are to your world. Your intention and attention give meaning and a sense of bonding power to all the matter around you. In any given moment, your thoughts, feelings, and actions affect everyone from your significant other to your children, from your coworkers to your friends. They, in turn, affect many others each day. The implications of this as it relates to your power and the influence you have on your world and all of the people in it on a daily basis are simply astounding.

A true understanding of time can be your greatest gift. It can change the way you look at how it all comes together for you. While there is a path of awareness needed to accumulate the conditions to make any dream or desire real, a new understanding of how your mind-set impacts matter, energy, and time can open up an array of new possibilities for you. You find that you have the power to change it all. **This golden opportunity exists for you, always, right now.**

YOUR ROLE IN THE
UNFOLDING OF INFINITY

So here you are forever at the center of life's journey of expansion into more and more possibility. You are now waking up to more of how the whole process of life works and what your role is within this process. You are a part of the expression of all possibility. You are one single point of consciousness within a sea of an infinite number of other expressions. Included in these expressions is everything you can see right now as you read these words. This includes all the people, places, and things around you.

Take a good, long look at all of it.

Every single bit of what you see in front of you is matter formed into different expressions of possibility, each serving a different intent. It is the content of the current state of consciousness organized into a certain context. It has all come from the millions of individual minds, thoughts, and intentions of everyone currently alive and everyone who has lived before you. **It has all come together in this moment for you as a demonstration of what is currently possible.** Whether it is the roof over your head, the chair you are sitting in, or the paper on which this book is printed, all of it is here to serve you.

What this all comes down to is the word *choice*. Your role, as granted to you by the nature of free will, is to endlessly choose how you will demonstrate who you believe you are. This is the root of it all. Your life is about using this free will of choice to create what you feel best serves you and your state of mind. A better understanding of you and your relationship to life, however, leads to more empowered choices!

It is not about how things *have* come together for you or how you *have* demonstrated yourself, but rather how you *will*, now in this moment, demonstrate yourself to your world. How will you demonstrate yourself to your spouse, significant other, boss, coworkers, customer, child, parent, stranger, or environment? How will you create from this moment and respond to each circumstance you face? Now is always your defining moment. What a wonderful opportunity you have before you.

> "The chief beauty about time is that you cannot waste it in advance. The next year, the next day, the next hour are lying ready for you, as perfect, as unspoiled, as if you have never wasted or misapplied a single moment in all your life. You can turn over a new leaf every hour if you choose."
>
> —Arnold Bennett

UNDERSTANDING THE CURRENT SYSTEMS OF LIFE

You cannot expect to harness your full creative power while simultaneously believing that you are limited by time or circumstance. You are a part of infinity. To the degree you feel that life is finite and limited, you will act out of this fear, and work to create an experience that is a result of this fear. Believing in a finite universe is a thought that works against the greater truth of the universe. By believing in limits, you set yourself on a course where life will bring pressure and suffering to these limiting thoughts, until a new, more open mind of possibility is the result.

At the same time you open to new possibilities, you must be keenly aware of the way that life has chosen to persist up until this moment. What I am referring to here is the reality of all the systems of survival formed by the collective consciousness that are already in place in your life and the life of all things around you. You must be aware of how to integrate with them for your chosen way of survival.

Examples of these systems of order include family dynamics,

your financial situation, the political system, the economic system, cultural systems, and the laws of the country in which you live and the legal system under which it operates. All of these systems and ways of regarding how life is managed and expected to operate must be acknowledged in order for you to:

1. Be in the most empowered and creative state of mind possible
2. Understand the full consequences of your choices and actions
3. Know how to best navigate the process of making your intentions a reality

IF YOU ARE UNAWARE or ignorant of how these systems of survival around you work, learning about them will take up some of the "time" you need to achieve what you desire. This learning curve can sometimes be very painful. This is why being aware of as much about these systems of life and the way they work as possible is key to enhancing your journey going forward from this moment.

The role you choose to play in life is really what you decide to make of it. A big part of making your journey as joy-filled and smooth as possible has to do with how aware you are of the way things work in life. Included in this is the way other people think, interpret, and feel. Understanding or not understanding the reactions of others around you and how they will respond to your choices will have a huge influence on how long your desires will take to manifest. The bottom line is that the price of ignorance is often suffering and the additional time needed to properly under-stand how to achieve what you want.

Just the state of being alive has certain requirements. Due to the mechanics of creation and evolution and the nature of change and movement, if you choose not to participate in the creative process of life, life will still move on without you. What will hap-pen is that you will eventually feel a loss of control. You will end up being dragged kicking and screaming as life pulls you around for a painful ride. If you choose to participate fully in life, and take the time to really understand more of how it works, however, your ride will be more comfortable and you will realize you have a massive influence on the direction it takes. And, last, if you try to force change (trying to get ahead of time), you will have to be very patient while you wait for your world and others in it to catch up with you. Whether you like it or not, you are in the play. You might as well take responsibility for as much of the writing of your character's story as you can. After all—you are the star.

> "Nature knows no pause in progress and development, and attaches her curse on all inaction."
>
> —GOETHE

HERE ARE SOME SIMPLE EXAMPLES of choices that are regres-sive and may not acknowledge the current realities of life and the systems of survival that have been put in place by the collective consciousness. Each of these choices is followed by a potential karmic consequence and time:

- You decide not to file taxes, so you experience IRS problems and penalties.
- You break the law, so you face legal repercussions.
- You choose not to face problems in your relationship, leading to mental and physical stress.
- You are ignorant to the state of political correctness at work, and as a result are held back from promotions, or even fired for seemingly small reasons.
- You don't eat healthy or you under- or overeat, which causes health issues.
- You are insensitive to your relatives or in-laws, creating relationship disharmony and family problems.

TO ACCOMPLISH WHAT YOU WANT in life you must be fully aware of what works and what doesn't work in each situation. Trying to lose weight by starving yourself is not the most optimal path to a healthy body. If you take your loved ones for granted and do not pay enough attention to their needs, your relationships can suffer. If you cut corners with your customers and fail to deliver as promised, they may end up favoring your competitors when you least expect it. If you ignore irregularities in your health and do not give your body's well-being enough attention, you could face serious health consequences when it is too late to do anything about it.

I could go on with other simple examples, but the point is that you cannot avoid the truth of the systems in place around you, and you must accept these truths initially in order to more quickly and more painlessly achieve what you creatively desire. This is a demonstration of the order of life and its precise ways. As you test these various systems, and they push back and protect themselves, you will see how heavily they factor in to determining your experience of time. Although many of these examples seem painfully obvious, what might not be as obvious is the way they delay your journey in life. The good news is that these systems and your awareness of how to maneuver your way through them can always change. This is the true purpose of learning experiences (mistakes), suffering, and pain.

On the other end of the spectrum, when you act in a progressive way that works to stretch the status quo or help a system to evolve, you also will experience pushback. In this case, however, there is the opportunity to move life in a way that may help expand the awareness of others, change hearts and minds, and lead to a more harmonious existence. Timing and readiness are key. You could:

- Exercise your right to vote
- Work to get a new law passed
- Present a new idea or way of thinking to society
- Invent a revolutionary new product
- Adopt a new energy of forgiveness, empathy, and trust with loved ones or family

WITH ANY PROGRESSIVE IDEAS, there is likely to be a certain amount of pushback or resistance, as the original systems in place try to keep things unchanged (family, friends, coworkers, politicians). Fear of the unknown is one of the strongest fears in the human psyche. Many new and revolutionary ideas that would immediately improve society are initially interpreted with great fear and therefore result in a powerful response of resistance from others, as history has continuously demonstrated.

Galileo's discovery that Earth revolved around the sun was not exactly met with cheers and open arms. The introduction of the electric car in the 1980s caused an entire auto industry to work to destroy it, and the institution of the civil rights bill in the United States was certainly met with fear and violent opposition by a large number of people who were very scared of change.

Ultimately, faith, belief, patience, and unwavering persistence by those working for positive change are what it takes to move any new idea along the path to becoming an accepted, new reality for all.

Knowing how to handle the systems around you when you seek change is extremely valuable in how you experience time during this process. The extent to which you are aware of the possible counterforce you can generate by your ideas or desires will help you as you move through the creative process. There will be less confusion and emotion when you do witness or experience potential resistance and opposition. This calm state will help you with the clarity and precise choices necessary to more seamlessly integrate and harmonize with the energy around you to accomplish what you imagine possible. **Ultimately, how you decide to deal with the ups and downs of any creative process is the single most powerful determining factor in how quickly things change in your world.**

THE PURPOSE
OF EVERYTHING

All the energy that you interact with each day is simply the expression of how consciousness has chosen to create and survive. These choices expressed in nature, individuals, countries, religions, political affiliations, and different societies as a whole have been put together and developed over thousands and thousands of years of action and reaction. What you are experiencing in your world is what for the moment is working in some way for a specific purpose. You may not be a particular fan of a religious order, type of music or cuisine, political opinions of family members, or a specific way that someone chooses to make a living. If it exists, however, there is an absolute reason for it. It is serving a purpose in the greater arrangement of life, or it would never have come into being.

Intention is the core word here. **There is an intention within the greater consciousness for everything in existence.** Your relative's addiction is not just a behavior meant to cause chaos for you and your family. A certain war is not happening just because of the choices of a few people. A currently incurable disease is not a random case of bad luck or the result of an angry God's wrath. This is not at all to trivialize these very heartfelt and emotional situations in life. **This is about offering the powerful awareness that everything happening in your view of life has a specific meaning for you.** There is a specific purpose for what is happening in each moment.

This type of thinking represents a fundamental shift of mind. It represents the dissolution of resistance. The experience of "time" is ultimately linked to your level of resistance or acceptance of what you experience. Therefore, it is an attitude of acceptance on your behalf that dissolves time and provides the greatest opportunity to change circumstance. It is critical that you know that the ending of your resistance toward any particular thing (sickness, layoffs, war, family, financial trouble, death, political chaos, natural disasters, etc.) is not in any way condoning these terrible things or giving up on change. It is simply the full acknowledgment that for the moment this is what *is* happening.

When this is fully understood, you see everything in your life in a different light. Again, this does not mean that you condone anything that does not align with your values or intentions. It does not mean you approve of certain parts of reality like war, death, evil acts, or deadly diseases. What it does mean is that you no longer question why any part of your reality exists but rather turn your attention to the much more powerful questions of "What can I learn from this?" "What is this circumstance trying to show me?" "How do I best deal with this challenge?" or "How can I work to change this or have a positive impact on this situation?"

In this very open and receptive state of mind, you accept the fact that a certain object or circumstance by its existence is enough of a demonstration of its purpose. From this more objective and clear state you can best choose how to deal with what is happening in a much shorter amount of time. Upon the moment of your acceptance you immediately begin to change the experience of time. This applies to any situation of life. Here are some examples.

FIGHTING YOUR significant other's negative attitude does not usually change it; in most cases, this simply makes it worse. Reducing your resistance and looking at it from the perspective that it exists for a reason allows you the opportunity to see the purpose of the behavior. This critical empathy does two things. One, it removes any sense of personal attack, which puts you in a less defensive and hence more empowered state of mind. And two, it helps you to see the best way to deal with the situation in order to effectively resolve the problem.

Getting angry and resisting your working conditions or pay may not change your situation at work, but may cause you to be labeled a problem employee. Accepting that the situation is, for now, the way it is, however, allows you to think of clear and smart actions to take that will lead to real change. Acceptance liberates your mind from the negative energy and emotion that creates "time." From a free, clear, and peaceful state of mind, you are able to be much more creative with your thoughts. This is what leads to the new choices or actions that actually change your circumstance.

On a more personal level, a few years back, my son, Jeffrey, who was eleven at the time, was having some trouble on his bus to and from school. He would come home a bit upset, and when pressed about it, he explained that there was a kid on his bus who picked on him and would never let him sit in the seat next to him when there were only a few open seats left. This caused some embarrassment for Jeffrey and forced him to sit in another area of the bus, far away from all of his friends. He felt angry, sad, and left out. He also did not understand why he was being treated this way by someone who was supposed to be his friend. As a parent, I obviously had a reaction of my own to the circumstances, but I also understood that this challenge presented a teachable moment—the opportunity for Jeffrey to learn a vital and important lesson at a very young age.

In the effort to help him, I asked, "Would you like to know how you might get this to change?" His immediate response was, "Yes," so I then asked him, "Did you do anything to upset this boy?" His answer was, "No." Next, I asked, "Do you feel good about the friend you are to him?" He responded, "Yes." So I told him, "This person's behavior is not about you. It has nothing to do with you. Reacting to it by getting upset was what he wanted. Be proud about who you are as a person and see if you can go a couple of days without needing to sit by him or without getting upset by anything he does, and let's see what happens."

When he came home the very next day, I asked him how it went. He said, "I got on the bus, walked down the aisle and passed by where he was sitting without even looking at him or asking to sit next to him." "What happened next?" I said. Jeffrey responded, "In less than a minute he came over to me, said 'Hi,' and asked me if I would sit next to him. He had never done that before."

In this very small incident, my son learned an incredibly pow-

erful lesson about his energy and how his response and the decision to let go of need affects his circumstance or the "time" the
situation he is in lasts. Even in a seemingly trivial experience like
this, his one small change in attitude, energy, and behavior gave
him an important glimpse into the real power he has in affecting
the behavior of others and in shaping his world of experience.

Think of it this way: The resistance you have toward any circumstance is a force of negative energy and actually helps in some
way to keep the circumstance alive. Have you ever really wanted
or, rather, needed someone to call you? This energy has a force associated with it that causes pressure. The person you desperately
want to hear from feels this pressure intangibly, and it has an impact on their actions. The minute you release the expectation or
need and "let it go" miraculously is the same instant the phone
rings; when you least *expect* it.

The negative energy of resistance is also what keeps you from
the balanced and focused state of mind that you require to make
more empowering choices. It's like splashing water in a pond, and
at the same time, trying to see the bottom of it. When you stop
fighting the truth of what is happening, relax, and let go of fear,
there is much more calmness and clarity of mind. This is when
the answers can easily be seen and found, and new positive actions
can be taken.

THIS WORKS THE SAME WAY for all the other circumstances or
events in your reality, including everything from traffic jams to
power outages, from health issues to financial trouble, from political turmoil to government corruption, from relationship trou-

bles to the job market or economy. Each scenario has a specific purpose and a very important role to play in your life. How you choose to respond to each circumstance is key to the power of your creativity and how fast you can change things.

What is fascinating and utterly transformational when you finally see it is the fact that whatever you are experiencing, or faced with in any given moment, is always for *you*. It is for you, your intentions, and your free will to decide how to deal with it as it relates to what you want for your life. You are creating the subjective experience of "time" by the way you perceive what you are experiencing and by the way you respond to your reality.

THE ACCEPTANCE OF INFINITY AS real and true and the understanding of your relationship to this truth are an essential foundation for the development of a new way to know and experience life and time. Time is not something you have or do not have, need or don't need, but rather something you determine and create by the way you deal with your world through every one of your thoughts and actions!

Waves

The ocean waves crash in
Never once the same
No care about the last
Free from memory and pain
Just to be
In each moment of eternity
Apart from conscious life
All the suffering all the strife
Re-creating in every moment
New is each day
The eternal message of life
The only thing there is to say
Pure experience is just being
Trying to repeat it is defeating
So be the change you are
Harmony is near not far
Perfection like the wave
Nothing ever out of place
Each movement like never before
Forever playing but keeping no score.

PART II

HOW YOU BECOME STUCK IN TIME

(Understanding Suffering)

> "How long a minute is, depends on which side of the bathroom door you're on."
>
> —ZALL'S SECOND LAW

WHY DOES IT SEEM TO TAKE SO LONG TO CREATE WHAT I DESIRE?

Everything you experience has taken a certain path of development to be in the form in which it is now. All the things in front of you have emerged out of something that developed before it, which has come forth from something before it, and so on and so on. The point is that there is a process to the emergence of everything in existence, including what you envision or dream about. This process is something you are in the middle of right now as you read these words.

For example, what any human being has accomplished throughout history started first from an intention. For this intention to manifest, there was a journey, a path of certain thoughts, feelings, and actions that produced the right conditions. Those who accomplished what they had originally intended took action on a path toward these intentions by relentlessly doing all that was necessary to achieve the end result. They learned through the course of the twists and turns of life what was needed to make their desire real. Each road traveled was different, each challenge unique, and each lesson particular to that person. The process, however, was the same for every one of them. This process is distilled in the following:

Intention → Questions → Awareness → Thought → Action → Result = Satisfaction?

If YES → The process is complete.

If NO → Re-establish Intention → New Questions → New Awareness → New Thought → New Action → New Result = Satisfaction?

If YES, the process is complete.

If NO, continue the process . . .

THIS SEEMS SO VERY SIMPLE when laid out on paper, doesn't it? It seems that if people would just follow the same formula, they would make their dream a reality. But this is not always the case. Why is it so different for so many millions of people? What is the separating factor? What is it that expands time in this process for so many and causes it to take almost no time for others?

What ultimately is at the core of any dream that becomes a reality is a strong will. This is a will that comes from a belief that says, "I believe in my intention, I will endlessly pursue my intention, and I will eventually make my intention real." This is a willingness to go through all the pain of roadblocks, missteps, tragedies, and

setbacks along the way. This is a will that pushes one to continue
to learn and move forward. One that never stops asking how to
take an idea in one's mind and turn it into a living reality.

**What "Will" Really Boils Down to Is
the Answers to the Following Questions:**

- How bad do you really want it?
- How much do you really believe in it?
- What are you doing right now to prove this to be true?
- How long are you willing to work at making it a reality?

THE ANSWERS TO THESE QUESTIONS are the determining factors in your experience of TIME as it relates to what you are trying to create or achieve.

So let's take a look at what the main issues are at the deepest
level of the mind that stretch time. Let's see what it is that causes
the creative process to slow down so that the amount of time involved feels longer and has you feeling stuck. Let's see what causes
one's "will" to become weak or ineffective.

TIME CREATOR #1:
REGRET OVER THE PAST

Since taking action is a big part of the creative process, any time not spent in active creation is time added to the process. One of the biggest ways to waste energy and stop creativity cold is through the belief in the destructive concept of regret. Not only is regret worthless to creativity, it's also personally destructive. It is a source of pain and a way to keep you from defining yourself in a new and more empowered way. "But I need regret so I won't make the same mistakes all over again!" is often a rationalization we use. It is used by the mind to hold you in a state of shame, blame, or imperfection. It is used to prevent you from stepping into a new identity and the feeling of fulfillment.

What is vital to remember from your previous experiences is the memory of how certain feelings and actions created a particular result. You need this information. For example, will choosing the same feelings and actions that you displayed in your previous experience serve you in the way that you wish to be defined now? This is the key question to ask yourself. Will yelling at your son or daughter out of frustration bring you any closer together? Will it build the love and trust that you are looking to create now? This is all that matters. Will lying to yourself about your job performance get you any closer to a new job or promotion?

Here is an example of the way regret impacts your choices, thus relating to "time" and how things unfold for you in life. Because of your regret over yelling at your child out of frustration the other day, you are now in a place where you need to relieve yourself of this horrible feeling. So you say to your seventeen-year-old, "I'm sorry, let me buy you something, take you out, help you do something, or get your forgiveness in some other way, shape, or form." Again, in this example you are coming from your *need* to feel better about your past actions instantly, not a true respect and understanding of your child's needs. It's like rushing to overwater a tree that you realize may have had years of poor nurturing. It doesn't work, and the rush to overwater it and "make up for lost time" may actually cause more damage.

Let's remember the original intention: to form a closer relationship built on love and mutual respect. Working from regret kills any chance of this occurring because it is action that is inauthentic. It is self-centered or need-based. The place from which a true connection is built is a place of mutual respect. One who has self-respect and an inner peace is one who is free of regret. When you come from this place of mind, you come without the need for something or someone to help relieve you of guilt. You are not trying to manipulate someone into doing something that makes you feel better. You are offering the comforting and sacred space of acceptance. The individual on the other end of the relationship no longer feels the pressure of making you feel better. They feel an authentic respect and in turn they value the relationship more and actually desire to deepen the connection.

The example above is one of many possible situations where regret limits your precious self-identity (I AM) and causes a delay in your true desires. Saying you shoulda, woulda, coulda done better in any part of your past is denial. There is only what you did— period—and it was always the very best you could do for that particular past moment. No other truth exists.

REGRET HAS NO POSITIVE VALUE. It is a concept used as a tool of manipulation. It does not change your behavior; it exacerbates it. If you hold on to any regret, it will poison your mind, body, or soul in another area of life. Any regret you've had must be dissolved for you to be free of the limits that it imposes on you. Subconsciously, regret limits what you feel you are worth, and it is part of what is creating the experience of time for you. **Creation happens only NOW. If you are mentally living in the past, you cannot simultaneously create something new and more positive.** The reason for this is that you are too busy resisting an act that already happened for you to be acting differently and more empowered now. Creation occurs only when you are absorbed purely in the present moment.

> "Try as they may to savor the taste of eternity, their thoughts still twist and turn upon the ebb and flow of things in past and future time. But if only their minds could be seized and held steady, they would be still for a while and, for that short moment they would glimpse the splendor of eternity, which is forever still."
>
> —SAINT AUGUSTINE

SO MANY LIVE in the place of denial and delusion. This state and the resulting pain that so many feel are evidence that we are all still learning. The purpose of any disappointment is for you to learn something that may help you on your path. This is life's process of awareness. Those who are master creators don't waste their time trying to change what they can't, or deny who they were, but rather, they actively work to learn from the past and use it in the only moment they have to redefine themselves anew: right NOW.

Accept that your past actions were based on who you were, not on who you are or who you can choose to be now. Accept this truth, and you will be free from regret forever.

TIME CREATOR #2:
FEAR OF THE FUTURE

Fear is one of the most debilitating, negative feelings you can experience. It is the single biggest reason for anxiety and disharmony in the world. Understanding fear's purpose and where it stems from is a huge part of taking control of it.

When you peel all the layers of the onion back on fear, you find that at the heart of it, fear is a message to you that your survival is in some way at risk. Survival in this case means the way in which you wish to experience your existence. So the fear of someone buying the company you work for really means, "Will they keep me on as an employee?" Fear of going to the doctor means, "Will there be something wrong with me?" Fear of meeting someone new on a date could mean, "Will they reject me?"

Fear is based on a projection of what *could* happen that is threatening to your survival. It is designed by the ego to keep you unchanged and in a space of what is "known" or "survivable" based on past history, no matter how much pain the situation has been causing you. **If you fear that a change to your situation will be**

worse than your current situation, you will not take any creative action.

A more dramatic example of this is a person who has an addiction that is destroying their life, their romantic relationships, their financial situation or their career, and their health. No matter how bad the destruction is, however, if the addict fears being worse off without the alcohol, drugs, etc., they will stay unmoved in terms of their choices and behaviors.

Change is the dirty word here. Fear often fills in the space that opens up when change is on the horizon. Over many years of transformation, the mind has found a way to protect itself from the idea or perceived threat of annihilation. This innate process where the mind is overprotective can become very dominating in your life and be a big reason that you may be unable to take the necessary steps you desire. Time then draws out as a result. You are left frustrated, impatient, and possibly feeling hopeless.

When looking at those who accomplish what they want in life we see a pattern emerge. People who succeed at their dreams do not let fear get in the way of their creative progress. **The key is they do not focus on what CAN'T be done but rather only see what CAN be done.** While it makes sense to be rational and clear about the inherent risks in moving forward with any creative endeavor, those who believe in themselves and the process of creativity will not let fear slow time down for them. They move boldly ahead with the creative actions necessary to build the conditions needed for their dreams to become reality. They don't think they will survive—they *know* they will.

A huge key in the process of mastering time is being able to recognize fear when it enters your mind and then being able to distinguish the truth from the lie it may tell you. By consciously stopping to recognize how a particular thought is holding you back, you put yourself in an empowered state to make a new choice about who you are and what you choose to believe in. **This is a tipping point in life. Will is a huge part of this. You can read this book about time and how it can affect your journey all day long, but until you are done watching the days go by without declaring a new identity and then taking the action to demonstrate this renewed self, not much will change in your reality.**

Nothing will change until you are done being trapped by your fears about moving forward with your life in some new way. Again, creation takes place in the present moment. If you are projecting a fearful future you are not creating now. There is great power in presence!

In the next twenty-four hours, you could take any of the actions listed below. If any of the following actions are related to your particular situation in life, watch carefully to see how your mind and body react to the idea. Watch the rationalizations, feelings, denials, and general projections of destruction that might pop into your mind upon the suggestion of these actions.

In the Next 24 Hours, You Could Easily:

- Print your résumé and send it to five different companies
- Sign up for an online dating service and e-mail a few people with matching interests
- Call your estranged in-laws, friends, children, wife, or husband and offer to start things anew

- Start writing the script or book you've wanted to write
- Have a much-needed "heart-to-heart" conversation with your significant other
- Put on your sweats and sneakers and go for a nice long run
- Empty your refrigerator and pantry of all the unhealthy food and restock it with healthy choices
- Set new rules of expected behavior and respect from your children
- Plan a spontaneous romantic evening with your significant other
- Develop a financial plan and budget that you will absolutely stick with
- Plan the vacation you have been dreaming about
- Start the paperwork for the business you've wanted to create
- Decide you are changing your attitude about fear and choose to live fearlessly and freely!

THE EXAMPLES ABOVE ARE just a few of the millions of action-based choices that you can make when you no longer let FEAR stop you. The choices above are what get the ball rolling and what begin to break the chains of TIME. **What keeps the ball rolling is something much deeper in you that knows that what you dream about achieving can become real.**

It is important to understand that taking action for the sake of taking action and proving you are overcoming your fear is absolutely worthless without a true will to accomplish the stated intention behind it. Time will find another way to be a part of your journey with this attitude. Another fear-based projection or situation will be manufactured in your life to delay the creation of the desire.

A dream without belief, will, and action will remain a dream.

So many of the fear-based reactions you feel are actually not based in fact. These are lies that you may have believed as true for many years. The question now is whether this way of thinking serves you and your current intentions. Do these beliefs about yourself or your world serve you and who you choose to be now? How strong of a will you have to stop "wasting" time will be evident in your next thought and action. Are you ready to end the painful experience of time that is created upon these old fears? Are you ready to enjoy something new? Only time will tell . . .

TIME CREATOR #3:
BELIEVING IN LIMITS

The most powerful mind is an open mind. What this really means is a mind that is not weighed down by old beliefs about what can't be done or what is not possible. This open mind is curious and willing to learn new information. This is the state of mind that has the best probability of creating what one imagines and dreams about.

Have you ever experienced "beginner's luck" or seen someone who has? It's an amazing thing to witness. Someone with no experience or little developed talent does very well in sports, business, gambling, relationships, the stock market, or other new "first-time" areas. This happens because they go into the experience with no memory or limiting expectations. Their mind is not projecting a bad outcome, and this open energy has a profound effect on what they create for themselves. Often this free and powerful energy of unlimited possibility leads to a successful result, at least for the first time! After that, projections and expectations may enter the mind and set one up for a potentially disappointing learning curve.

From a young age, many of us are programmed or influenced by our caregivers, primarily our parents, as to what is possible in the world. Before we fully know our name, we are being told "No" and shown boundaries. When we were children, our first idea of what is possible came from what we saw in our parents' lives. **We tend to believe early on that the life our parents lead is the way life is supposed to be lived.** As we grow older, we see others achieving different outcomes and living differently, so our view begins to expand and change.

The biggest factor that drives the experiences of life is the way in which we view ourselves. This is what really sets the limits we create and believe in. Once these limits are set in our mind and identity (I AM), we will do everything possible to make sure that these limits become a reality. The nature of life is what drives us to take what we believe to be true and make sure it becomes a reality. Every thought, feeling, and action is involved in this process. Therefore, identifying where our limits are and what we believe is true are huge parts of identifying where we are slowing down time for ourselves.

The ego is your bridge between thought and reality. It allows you to know who you are from an experiential standpoint. It works with your self-identity to make sure that what is believed to be true is defended, protected, created, and validated. By observing the actions of your ego rather than resisting it, you are in the best position to see what truths or limits your ego is trying to serve.

That is when you are most empowered to change these beliefs. You must become acutely aware of the instructions your ego has been receiving and working to serve so you can finally consciously take control and change them.

The limits we each hold about what is possible for us are a key factor that influences time. What is interesting is that we will often still go through the motions to try and create something for ourselves, even though at a deep level, we don't believe it is possible. Most of the time life proves these limits to be correct for us and nothing happens. Every once in a while, however, life surprises us and produces what we didn't believe possible. By demonstrating some morsel of faith in taking action, we were graced with this new life-changing and belief-changing result, like buying a lottery ticket and—to your surprise—actually winning something, or putting your name in for the promotion at work you thought you had no shot at and actually getting it.

The following are some examples of damaging and limiting beliefs and how they influence the "time" it takes to experience a larger intention or desire.

A belief at a deep level that there is a limit on how long someone will tolerate you or love you, in many cases, will still allow you to go through the motions of being in a relationship, getting married, or even having children. These beliefs, however, will ultimately lead to a troubled relationship, or may even cause the relationship to end in divorce if this limit is not discovered and changed. If you hold on to any limiting beliefs about being loved, you will inevitably either subconsciously or consciously try to "prove" the limits to be true and find a way to sabotage your relationship. The "time" it will take to create a truly loving and lasting relationship will be deeply affected by this limit, until the limit is discovered, seen as no longer true, and then changed.

A belief that you can't make more than a certain amount of money or that you can't rise above a certain economic level will surface in a situation where you are fast-tracking your career but suddenly put a stop to it. You may do something out of the ordinary or make a certain decision that brings all your momentum to a halt. Many well-known actors, actresses, musicians, and athletes may come to mind when thinking about this form of self-sabotage. They simply hit a wall in their level of success because at a deep, subconscious level, they believed nothing more was possible for them. The limits of their own minds were on full display in some of the head-turning actions and events that led to their downfall from the dazzling heights they had reached—the proverbial fall from grace. The perfection of the design of life to match with personal truth and identity was on display in their self-destructive behavior. One's truth must ultimately rule the day, regardless of how much of a "waste" it seems or how confusing it may be to others. Clearly these celebrities would have made different choices had they been at peace with their success and who they believed they were.

Our beliefs about our health and, even more specifically, our weight can have certain hidden limits that work on our experience of "time." Sometimes it's deep beliefs about self-worth and vulnerability that work to keep the weight on as a form of protection, and other times it's simply a belief that it is hard to lose weight or

difficult to avoid the temptation of certain foods that is really
what is responsible for the time it takes to lose the weight. We do
our best to live out the truth of any perceived limit.

The diagram below displays how your identity determines
your intention and the limits of your intention. The experiences of
these limits are then precisely cultivated in your reality. Inside the
boundary line indicates where your comfort zone resides. Excuses
or rationalizations are among the many tools the ego uses to keep

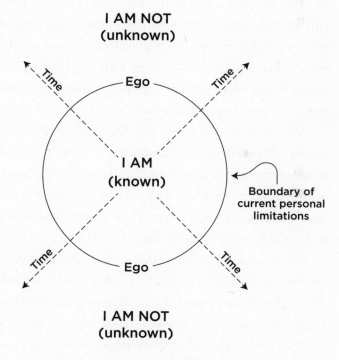

Everything outside the circle is the field of
unlimited possibilities yet to be experienced.

this identity line intact in this visual example. Until you are ready for the information that will create change in you, the ego will vigorously defend these limits.

EVERYTHING INSIDE THE CIRCLE (I AM) is what is known as survivable and comfortable. The ego's job is to guard this line between the unknown and known. It is designed to protect and defend all the current beliefs (I AM) and prevent change. It does this by projecting a fear of the unknown. The only time the ego will work to push out the boundary line or circle is when new desired personal intention, combined with a strong will, becomes powerful enough to overcome the fear, enabling change and the ability to step into a new identity. Time collapses and transformation occurs as a new I AM is born.

All of your dreams, hopes, and desires are outside of the circle. Belief, will, trust, and faith are what work to expand the circle outward toward these dreams, into new creative experiences, a greater consciousness, and hence, a new identity. It is about moving beyond your comfort zone. Time is a measure of this creative process as it continually expands.

One example of moving beyond your comfort zone would be the first time you gave a speech in school or had to speak in front of a large group of people. Public speaking represents one of the biggest fears people have in life. Many are not comfortable with being so vulnerable and exposed when a whole lot of eyeballs are focused on them at once. If your current identity circle does not include speaking in front of people, speaking to a crowd for the first time can cause quite a bit of anxiety, as the ego has to deal with the fear of a new level of attention and exposure. The greater the level of insecurity, the more terrifying it will feel to speak. If the will is strong enough, however, it can power you through the experience, dry mouth, shaky legs, and all.

From that one breakthrough moment on, each time you speak, it will get easier and easier, as you become comfortable with your new identity as a public speaker. Any new experience can be terrifying, as the ego grapples to deal with an unknown experience. For any change you attempt, going from known to unknown takes faith in your ability to step into a space that feels uncomfortable.

The ease or difficulty of what you need to do next are always relative terms based on your will. What seems hard for one person who lacks the will is very easy for another who sees it as an inevitable part of who they desire to become. While one goes through life in fear with their foot on the brake of creativity, another who has more faith has no problem putting their foot squarely on the creative accelerator.

In the vehicle of personal creation, belief is the ignition, will is the engine, and faith is the fuel that keeps it all moving.

So the million-dollar question is "Where does personal will come from?" The answer is highly personal and a combination of three things: a belief in oneself, a strong active desire, and an unwavering faith in the outcome of the process. Will is demonstrated when all three of these things are present.

As we have seen on recent reality shows dealing with losing large amounts of weight, the time it takes to lose the weight cor-

responds with the will and consistent action of the person involved. **Therefore, time is relative to intention.** While there are
some current physical laws of possibility (the ability to lose weight
and keep it off) or the ability to do anything in a certain time
frame (like demolishing and completely rebuilding and refurnish-
ing a house in two weeks), it is up to the participants, the focus of
their intentions, and what limits they are willing to challenge and
look beyond.

**Time is not something you have or don't have; time is some-
thing you make.**

ON THE PATH TO BECOMING a master of time, it is important
to understand where your limits have come from, how they have
affected your creative endeavors, and the impact they have had on
your journey thus far.

ANOTHER AREA TO WATCH OUT for as it relates to setting limits is the opinion of other people in your life. If I had a dollar for
every person who told me what couldn't be done . . . You get the
point. Others will impose their own fears and limits on you, especially when you are doing something that is beyond what they
believe to be possible. This is not because they are mean-spirited
or sinister but because they are trying to confirm that what they
believe about life is still true. They have their own personal limi-
tations, and oftentimes, they do not want to see that another way

actually exists. They may be afraid of the reflection on their own life if you succeed. It will force them to reevaluate what they believe to be possible.

When you are on the path to making your desires real, make sure to stay steadfast in your powerful beliefs and to watch out for the negative influence of other people and their attempts to hold you back.

Remember, life is here to serve you and what you believe to be true. Your beliefs about what is or is not possible will be demonstrated both consciously and subconsciously through every one of the ways you distract yourself, procrastinate, or delay the creative process. To gain more creative control you must recognize this behavior. Any self-imposed limit in your mind will only add to the time it takes to realize any desired creative experience on your continuing journey of life.

> "It is not enough to be industrious; so are the ants. What are you industrious about?"
>
> —Henry David Thoreau

TIME CREATOR #4:
PROTECTING FALSE BELIEFS

Awareness is change. You've probably heard it before that a mind once stretched never goes back to its original size. When new information comes into your awareness, and it always will, it changes who you are and it becomes much harder to hide under the rock of ignorance. It is as if life forces us to live in more of the current truth no matter how hard the ego works to hold on to the old, outdated beliefs about life. Truth is so much more powerful than falsehoods. The ego will eventually exhaust itself in the effort to defend what is not working anymore and will finally submit to the new, unavoidable reality.

Until this exhaustion takes place and the will becomes strong enough to create change, however, even the deepest of our desired prayers will seem unanswered. This is because the ego will purposely avoid what life is divinely presenting. This is a big part of what seems to slow down the creative intentions of millions of people. They ask questions, in their mind, to God, to the universe, and to others, and the universe responds right on cue. **The ques-**

tion is not whether the universe has answered you; the question is always, are you ready to finally listen?

WILLFUL IGNORANCE IS AN ASTONISHING part of the process of the unfolding of time in life. It is remarkable how the ego can work to protect you from the truth by blocking information, rationalizing it, and downright reshaping it to avoid what is really being offered. We see it in religion, science, politics, business, spirituality, and just about every way people choose to look at the world. The process has its perfection. The mind can only open to and absorb as much new information as your will—or your "soul"—will allow. If what you ask to understand means having to accept information that will stretch your consciousness to a place that you are not fully ready to explore or are fearful of experiencing, you will rationalize it, denounce it, or find a way to completely avoid it, no matter how liberating the information is.

Have you ever tried to offer help or information to someone in a tough situation who simply wasn't ready to change? Regardless of the pain of what they are going through, the fear of change will rear its head in different ways to protect them from the truth if they aren't ready for it. It doesn't matter how many times you tell them or how badly their life is crumbling; your words will go in one ear and out the other. It can be exhausting to try and offer positive, life-changing information to someone who clearly does not show the readiness or "will" to change his or her circumstance.

The way information is ignored by the mind is revealed in the following tools of the ego. Each of these ways of blocking new information increases or "stretches" the experience of time as it relates to the desired goal or creative intention:

- **Denial:** non-recognition of information in order to avoid its message
- **Delusion:** the reshaping of information to avoid the message it is offering
- **Contempt:** holding someone else responsible for the information to avoid being held accountable to the message
- **Judgment:** declaring someone wrong to avoid what is being presented

Examples Include the Following:

- You ask why your relationship is not fulfilling, but you do not want to acknowledge your own fear of communicating your feelings, being vulnerable, or facing some previously avoided truths with your partner. When someone confronts you about your walls, you immediately defend yourself, change the subject, or ignore them completely.
- You wonder why you always struggle with money, but yet you rationalize many of your frivolous purchases and avoid getting control of your spending habits. This is done to avoid the truth that you are handling money poorly, and perhaps avoid the underlying issue that you have felt unworthy of having money.
- You ask why you haven't been promoted at work, but avoid the truth that the company you work for is looking to downsize, not to promote from within. Instead of seeing this truth

(that you should seek employment with another company to advance your career), you hold your boss in contempt and say he or she is trying to keep you down on purpose or you rationalize that career opportunities don't come your way.

- You say you want to eat healthier and become more fit, but blame others for causing you the stress that leads to overeating and poor exercise habits. You also say you don't have the time to exercise and eat healthier rather than choosing to take the time and make these significant and healthy changes.

The ego, as the loyal protector and defender of your identity and existence, will use any trick in the book to keep you away from new truths, in the effort to keep you within your known comfort zone. The ego will do this until your soul crosses the threshold of tolerance and moves to a place of *intolerance*. Then, and only then, will your will and ego submit and overcome your fear long enough to allow the necessary information into your awareness. This is what will end a part of your ignorance and lead to a new identity (I AM). A new identity is what allows new understanding, thoughts, feelings, and actions. This is the sequence of events and the real mechanics behind the collapse of time, as new conditions arise, leading to a new reality.

TIME CREATOR #5:
THE FORCE OF NEED

When you get comfortable with a certain way of living and doing things that has become identified as necessary for your survival, any threat to this way of living can often be seen as a threat to your very existence. When you are threatened with change or loss, need becomes the predominant feeling. The energy generated by the feeling of need ironically does not help you get any closer to what you want but rather pushes what you want farther out on the spectrum of time. The degree of fear behind your need is the core of the negative force at work. There is nothing wrong with wanting or desiring something. The difference with need when it comes to creating is that you are starting from fear and a belief in "Not good enough." Or "Not survivable." This false destructive energy then gets in your way. Here are some examples:

- You *need* a romantic relationship. If, when you are dating, this need is the predominant feeling you have, this neediness on your part will eventually be felt energetically by the other person in the form of pressure, and this may actually drive that person away from you.

- You *need* to get the job. If you lack faith in yourself and your abilities, and are desperate for the new job, this need will come through in interviews as either overconfidence or a severe lack of confidence. Those interviewing you may feel this energy, and this can end up causing them to pass over you for the job.

- You *need* to look good and be noticed in a positive way. If you feel you need to be in shape and noticed to such a high degree that you push your body to extremes or overuse plastic surgery, this need may actually cause physical fatigue and a loss of objectivity regarding your true beauty and attractiveness. The result is that you actually end up drawing negative attention to yourself.

THE REASON WHY NEED CAN be so damaging and actually add painful time to the creative process is that need comes from a mind-set that says things like, "I will not be able to survive without this amount of money," or "I won't be able to go on without that particular person in my life." **If this is your believed truth, your ego will work to actually create the experience of this truth.**

When fear and need are present in your mind, they work on your psyche in a way that prevents you from creating the conditions that would allow you to have what you want. If there is more energy in the fear of not having something in your life than there is energy in the faith that it is possible for you to have it, it will tip the scale of universal probabilities and build the conditions toward it not happening. **The universe can only conspire with you regarding what you really believe to be true.** This is an extremely important recurring theme in this book. Any fear you have in your mind demonstrates a truth you hold. The universe responds in the effort to either make the believed fear a reality, or to show you that the fear you have believed to be true is actually false. Fear in many cases can be very self-fulfilling—dwelling on certain fears can end up manufacturing the conditions that lead to the very things you want to avoid.

The key to creating what you want sooner is to keep the desire and the belief in what is possible for yourself while at the same time dropping any strong need for these possibilities to manifest.

Need does not come from a powerful place of mind or produce a state of power. It comes from a place of fear and force. It originates from a lack of faith. It may seem like a paradox to say this but **to be in the greatest place of power, you must detach from what you think you need to get what you truly want.**

The greater truth is that your most potent power comes from a true faith in a perfect universe. You already are complete in this moment. Do we all have certain basic needs for survival? Yes. Do we all have creative desires and intentions? Yes. This is the primal creative urge of life and the ongoing process of the demonstration of infinity. However, when it comes to being a master of your reality, having full trust in the great conscious creator that you are and in the self-supporting universe around you is a quantum leap in awareness and true wisdom.

. . .

UNDERSTANDING WHAT KEEPS YOU STUCK in the experience of time is a huge key in the process of conscious creation. As you become more aware of when you are trapped in your past, fearful of your future, and working against your intentions, you begin the climb out of the wheel of time. When you realize that you are operating out of an old limit or belief, and when you become aware of your false fears, you can finally be empowered to take charge of time and change the way things come together in your life. No longer in a state of ignorance or denial, you know exactly what is keeping you from creating the conditions for any dream that you have for your life. There is no going back under the rock. You are revealed as the full commanding captain of your vessel. Welcome to a fully conscious life. Time is now finally on your side.

Once Again

Minutes turn into hours
Hours meld into days
Days to weeks and months
What is it that holds me from the vision in my mind?
What thoughts have worked against me and my precious dreams?
What unseen force lay upon my chest and a full breath?
Regardless, I will not relent
For my will is strong
My spirit full
My soul awake
No obstacle will block my path
No ill thought will go unchallenged
No limit will ever become real
For I have learned the source of time
I have become wise to its power
I walk unafraid to know, willing to lose it all
Past and future dissolve
And thus the power of creation fills me
Beauty and perfection revealed
The glorious eternal moment is now mine once again!

PART III

HOW TO DISSOLVE TIME AND CREATE WHAT YOU DESIRE

(Awakening to the Beauty of the Process)

> "Who controls the past controls the future. Who controls the present controls the past."
>
> —GEORGE ORWELL

HOW TIME EXPANDS
AND CONTRACTS

Every one of your intentions has a certain timetable that it follows to its realization. This timetable is determined in large part by the energy of your will to see the intention realized. Throughout your life, you have had millions of conscious and subconscious thoughts in the form of desires, wishes, hopes, dreams, and needs. Each of these thoughts had and continues to have a certain amount of energy attached to it. You incessantly followed up on some of these thoughts until you created them. Others may have started with strong intentions on your behalf, but did not have enough energy behind them to come to fruition. Eventually the energy propelling some of these old intents simply dissipated, and as a result no part of your feelings or actions moved you to work further to make them a reality.

With many of these intentions, you either lost interest, never followed up on them, or failed to persevere long enough. The belief behind some of them was simply not strong enough. Also, as life evolves and changes, intentions can change as new, more pressing desires emerge.

When you break it down, "personal will" becomes the driving factor behind which intentions you focus on experiencing and how fast you learn what you need to do to accomplish them. For example, when it comes to the primal intents to eat, sleep, or find a bathroom, we make it a priority that these things are accomplished. **Time in this sense is directly related to the will to turn intent into reality. The link between the two is awareness.** The shorter the learning curve, the shorter the time it takes to achieve your dream. Again, will is the determining factor. Time can seem to expand when you make a poor choice that sets you back, or time can contract and feel as if it's speeding up when you feel you are making progress. A key part of mastering time and life is discovering how your state of mind affects how quickly you accept new information. We each have a filter in our mind that governs how fast our consciousness expands and thus how time gets paced. The filter is governed by pure will and desire.

The information you are looking for is already here for you. It has always been here for you. How you actually experience time as it relates to what you want to know depends on your readiness to see these new answers and allow them into your consciousness. Part of the elegance of the universe rests in the understanding that the timetable surrounding this process is a product of your free will. I assure you that when you are absolutely ready for answers, the universe will flood you with them. It will lay them at your feet.

Life is constantly showing you the difference between what you say that you want and who you demonstrate that you are.

. . .

THERE IS PERFECTION IN THE design of life. Each human being paces time and the awareness that comes with it in a way that is tolerable to them. That is why trying to force someone to do something or be someone that they are not ready to be can be a very daunting task. This is a task that is usually met with a very forceful resistance. The only exception is when they actually show a genuine interest in change and ask for help—when they have a will strong enough to allow for change. Each person has to be ready for how any new attitude and actions are going to change their identity.

Examples of this can range from trying to help a friend or loved one break an addiction to telling them that their relationship is unhealthy. While they may show a desire for change, they may not be anywhere near ready for change. If so, be prepared for strong resistance to what you are offering. The evolution of awareness, or time, is a very personal and highly protected journey. Knowing this will help you to be more effective when you are with them.

The way in which you communicate with people you are trying to help is very important. When you judge them, pressure them, or try to manipulate or coerce them to change, what you are really saying to them is "Who you are being right now is not good enough." Ironically, this opinion plays right into their negative story. This is the reason they're having trouble in the first place. Their own limited identity has produced their current circumstance. Your condemnation is actually telling them in so many words that the low self-image that they have about themselves is something you believe to be true as well.

Rather than condemn them, a much more effective way to help them is to recognize the self-evident truth that for the moment, they are doing the best they can. This doesn't mean you condone their behavior or let yourself be manipulated by them, but if you can truly shift your perspective and see them differently, this new energy will have an immediate positive effect. It will shift the way they respond to you and even how they respond to themselves.

Use your words to lift the spirits of others and you help free them from the chains of mind and time.

THIS HAS TO BE a genuinely new way of looking at them that is free of judgment. This must come from a place of greater understanding and love. This also has to be done with great respect for their personal free will. This is the true process of having an impact on anyone looking for change.

When our hopes and dreams take a long time to come to fruition, or when it seems like we are not making any progress at all, we tend to rationalize our situation by telling ourselves that life gets in the way or that we are victims of circumstance. What is happening in many of these cases is that our true beliefs in who we are and what's possible for us ultimately are ruling the day. These limiting thoughts end up becoming roadblocks that we use as greater excuses for why things are the way they are. They add to the layers. The longer this goes on, the more the drama of our particular experience can become an impediment to achieving what we want.

"I just *can't* do this."

"It will *never* happen."

"I'll *always* be like this."

"I just *have* bad luck."

These statements are all untrue. These are just a few of the lies that run through the mind of someone who lacks the readiness or determination to accomplish what they desire. It is evidence that they do not have a strong enough belief in themselves or in the attainability of their goals.

"In order to be a realist you must believe in miracles."

—David Ben-Gurion

Of course there are some much larger mountains to climb and bigger challenges to face in terms of your specific intent, but when you have a strong will and belief in yourself, and when you're grounded in a true understanding of how everything in your life is connected, all becomes possible. Words like *can't*, *never*, and *always* aren't used anymore, and these old excuses are revealed for the lies that they are.

At the most fundamental level, everything is composed of energy, so we are each tethered to everything in existence in some way, shape, or form. This is a very important understanding as it relates to trusting the process of creation. When you begin to move in the direction of your intention, many other people, places, and things begin to come together, to line up and help you fulfill that particular idea.

What is interesting is that if your intention is not in line with the greater will of the collective consciousness or your actions finally lose favor with the majority of minds around you, all of life will come together to resist, repress, or destroy your idea or intent. This truth is never more evident than in the final days of so many fallen dictators or oppressive regimes in the world over recent years. Eventually life always reveals where you stand as it relates to the greater truth around you.

One of the most powerful realizations you can come to on your journey of awareness is that the universe is here to serve *you*. This is not some egotistical notion of specialness or separateness, but something much more empowering and profound. Life serves the continuation of life. When your intention is unified in serving the greatest number of hearts and minds, the power of the universe is behind you. When these intents are most destructive as it relates to life, the universe works to reveal this ignorance by pressure and destruction. This is a realization that our most deeply held thoughts and truths are where we direct all the energy of our creative actions.

Think of anybody you know right now. You will see how much their current actions reveal what is most important to them. We are each driven to validate our beliefs and discover new ways to demonstrate our existence. What is interesting is that once we know something to be absolutely true, we no longer need to validate it. Our energy is only directed at what we question and that which expands our awareness of the nature of who we are. This is how life unfolds and why everybody is on the very same general quest. That is why so many of the right players, performers, and portrayers sync up with you when you are on a path that serves them as well and why so many resist you when your intentions are not in harmony with their own.

Your energy is driven by the creation of I AM. Your most deeply held truth must be validated in your reality. This is how life works at the core.

Mind must become matter. I must become AM. You must know I AM experientially.

YOU ARE CONSTANTLY NUDGED TO experience your own existence through the process of thoughts becoming real. Not being able to experience yourself as intended—I AM—will draw out time and be the cause of some degree of suffering. This will continue until you are either able to experience yourself as you wish, or until you simply accept the truth that right here and right now you are good enough exactly as you are.

Not to worry. You will always find a way to survive. The binding power of unconditional love that is behind existence cannot, has not, and will not have it any other way. You will continue to be nurtured along the necessary and sometimes challenging path of awareness. This is really what everything in existence (including this book) is helping you through. The universe does not always partner with you to fulfill your deepest dreams and desires. Rather, the real treasure is the precious awareness that the universe is working to deliver to you in so many different ways, always leading you to a greater knowledge of what *is* possible for you.

> "We don't wish, we know; we don't dream, we state; we don't hope, we accept; we don't pray, we announce."
>
> —ANONYMOUS

WHEN YOU DECLARE any strong intention, you will immediately begin to receive feedback from the world related to "how?" Life's response will be to show you this necessary awareness continuously until you acknowledge it. **This path of awareness is the essence of the purpose of time.**

How Many Times Did You:

Fall off your bike when you were learning to ride it?

Experience heartbreak in a relationship until you knew exactly what you wanted?

Lose or change jobs in order to find the right one?

Drink too much until you learned not to overdo it and make yourself sick?

We learn, we adapt and we evolve. Our experiences and setbacks show the way.

LIFE IS A SEA of constant change, and it requires an ever-changing awareness in order to stay in the creative flow. Fall out of touch with the current consciousness and you get stuck in time. Have you ever known someone who always wants it to be "like it used to be"? Someone who refuses to accept the changing times and new ways of living? The use of texting and the incredible new way this communication medium has taken over so much of our world is a great example here. Many resist this method and wonder why people (especially kids) can't talk to one another like they used to. The reality is that this is what an entire generation has developed and chosen as a new form of communication and socialization. It is clearly a medium of exchange that is here to stay for a while. For those unwilling to accept the use of texting or any other significant changes that take place, the world can feel assaultive and they can often experience the feeling that they are slipping behind the times.

The point is, our state of awareness is directly relatable to "time" in all aspects of our life. It is related to what we have created, what we are creating, and, most important, what we will create. Creation is most powerful when we are in harmony with the truth of the powerful consciousness of Now.

How time dissolves for you as it relates to what you want comes down to three main variables: the strength of your will to obtain new information, the degree to which you believe in yourself, and

the amount of perseverance you demonstrate through your actions. These three aspects (awareness, belief, and action) determine your level of faith in what is possible for you. This is the fuel
that will drive the magic of the creation process—the journey of
gaining awareness and putting, or rather *pulling*, all the necessary
conditions together to achieve your dreams.

"Pulling" is actually the appropriate term here because your
intention, will, and faith will pull the new people, places, and
events together that are required to give life to your ideas. It all
depends on how connected your intention is to everyone else's in
your world. **The more your existence and actions serve others
and are in synchronicity with their intentions, the faster it will
all come together for you.**

An example of the creative and synchronistic side of this process
is seen in the recent success of Apple. Apple rocketed to success in
the last ten years because the intention for computers, cell phones,
and other digital devices that are easy to use, have a cool design,
and are very reliable grew enormously for millions of people. Many
were completely fed up with the continuous Control-Alt-Delete
process to reboot a frozen PC. This synchronicity all came together and merged with Steve Jobs's vision and incessant intention
to produce extremely well-built, well-designed, and very cool products. Time has certainly collapsed for this company, in terms of
how quickly they have developed and sold new, reliable, and revolutionary computers and cell phones to an extremely loyal customer base.

On the destructive and disharmonious side of the spectrum, the
eventual fall from power and death of Muammar Gaddafi in 2011
represented a growing discontent and disconnection for a majority

of the people of Libya and around the world. Gaddafi ruled Libya for forty-two years, until the greater will of the people forced him from power. Years of political abuse and a profound disconnect from the will of the people of Libya and a majority of the world came to a boiling point in the fall of 2011. In this case, the longer the intention and will of Gaddafi did not serve the greater will of those over whom he presided, the more this truth made its way into his awareness. The speed of his downfall was in direct proportion to the degree of ignorance and resistance to the truth of the opposing needs and desires of the people. Gaddafi remained defiant almost until the end of his leadership. Truth spares no one. No matter what is happening in the world now, rest assured that the greater will of the collective consciousness will ultimately prevail in what gets created, changed, and supported next.

This process is no different on an individual level, especially when it comes to your relationships, your job, or any intention you are looking to create or continue experiencing. Staying keenly observant of the current state of awareness is a huge key to the power of your ability to experience what you want. There is a price to pay for remaining in a state of ignorance. That price is found in time and suffering. Your heart and desire, however, will always carry the day. While time and a certain degree of suffering may be a significant part of creating something new, staying steadfast and determined in your vision and working toward what is possible will prove to be a very important part of the process of faith and the beautiful results you generate.

Expanding time versus collapsing time (speeding up the creation of what you intend for your life) comes down to your answers to the following questions. Take your time as you go through each one of these to see where you are in the process. Read the questions, ponder your responses, and if you are really serious about your answers, write them down after each question.

- Do you have a strong intention to make your idea or dream real?
- Do you believe your intention is possible for you?
  If no, why not?
- Do you have a strong will to see your intention realized?
  If yes, what five things have you done in the last week to create this intention?
- Are you asking the important questions each day of HOW?
- Are you listening to your reality for the answers?
- Are you honoring the true feelings of others in your life or are you dominating them with your needs?
- Are you actually creating change by making new choices?
  If no, what holds you back?
  If yes, what new choices have you made in the last month?
- Do you trust that life is always serving you on your quest?
  If no, how do you see life working against you?
- Can you see the creative process in action right here in this moment as you read these words?
- Do you understand what you have created in your past and why you have created it?
- Are you ready to face new challenges?
- Are you acting from a place of personal peace, acceptance, and love?
  If no, why not?

. . .

THESE ARE VERY IMPORTANT QUESTIONS to ask yourself as you move toward what you want to accomplish.

Ninety-nine out of a hundred requirements for what you desire may already be fulfilled; yet all it takes to keep the whole experience from happening is one bit of self-doubt saying "no."

The list of questions above may be something you want to keep referring back to. They provide a great way for you to see where you stand in any given moment in relation to what you want for your life.

THE POWER OF THE PRESENT moment has been discussed quite a bit lately in much of the material available on manifesting and attracting that which you desire. Over the last several years, meditation has been the most popular path offered by much of the self-help movement to help get you into the present moment. It has been presented as the way to quiet the mind and end distracting thoughts. While this is a wonderful exercise and process that has helped many, there is another way to approach being present that may have a different and very lasting effect.

A mind full of chatter is acting in this way for a specific reason. To avoid this reason is to distract yourself from an important point of growth and evolution. There are two main factors that cause a lack of presence of mind: focusing on resisting your past; or projecting an undesired reality for the future. Remove both of these distractions, and presence becomes a daily state of living.

THE PERFECTION
OF THE PAST

Oh, how we've all experienced moments that we would like to go back and change! How different our lives would be if that were possible. "If only" is a constant thought revisited by many people who are stuck in time. "If only I had taken that job, gone to school, loved them more, not made that investment, controlled my temper, sold that house, listened more," and on and on . . .

Focusing on changing the past is focusing on an illusion. That time no longer exists. All you have is now. Using your mind in this particular way does not serve you in a positive way. All that this type of thinking does is slow time. It keeps you stuck in a type of purgatory where you cannot change anything and you cannot create anything. It robs you of the power of the moment and the beautiful experiences you can create by becoming more present. You cannot change what already happened, but you always have the opportunity to change the way you look at, feel about, and identify with what happens in this instance now. This could be one of the most powerful points in this book.

You are not who you were but who you choose to be right now.

YOUR PAST ACTIONS AND EXPERIENCES may have defined you up until now, but they do not have to define you from this moment forward. The power of choice (I AM) is eternally yours. **Declaring who you are is the most important choice you can make because it determines all of the thoughts, feelings, and actions that you will put out to the world, and it divinely and precisely determines how the energy of your universe responds to you each and every second.** It determines what opportunities come your way, how others treat you, what they say to you, and how you feel about it. It is the cornerstone for all that unfolds for you.

Looking back at your past and being able to see the perfection of it is imperative, as it relates to your personal growth and evolution. "If I only would have listened to myself or simply not done what I did." Woulda, coulda, shoulda. Three of the biggest lies in existence. They are simply tools of the ego to prevent an expansion of your awareness that is the bedrock for positive transformation and change. This is all directed by an "I" or a mind that is trying to validate some idea of yourself that says I AM regretful, I AM stupid, or I AM not good enough in some particular way. These poisonous thoughts must be cleared out to be able to make a more powerful choice now.

Living in the past is draining and tiresome. Whenever you choose to avoid truth, it takes a certain amount of energy to resist it. Wishing the past to be different drains you, as your soul fights a greater truth. The path to liberation is to see the perfection of your past. "How in the world can hurting someone, destroying a relationship, or making a choice that led to financial ruin be perfect?" you may be asking. The answer requires a new way to look at the word "perfect."

When I refer to the *perfection* of every choice and action of your past, I am not saying that it was the desired choice, or the one with the most peaceful and pleasant outcome. **The decisions you made in the past were always the reality of the best you could have done *for that particular moment* and were divinely necessary for everyone involved. If your decision created chaos, it was necessary for your journey. It was how life chose to get your attention, shed some awareness, and put you exactly on the path that you are on today.**

The simple, powerful, and unavoidable truth is if you could have done better anytime, anywhere, you would have.

THERE IS NO OTHER TRUTH. "But I knew better," you might say. If you knew better, however, why didn't you choose better? Your actions in any past moment always demonstrated what you felt you needed to do at that particular moment, or they demonstrated the limits of your awareness concerning the consequences of your actions.

There is no going back, only the infinite opportunity of choice that is offered to you right now. Knowing this and actually stepping into this truth could free you forever.

WHAT INCREDIBLE POWER IS AVAILABLE to you in this moment! How exciting is it to know that releasing yourself from the illusion of woulda, coulda, and shoulda frees you and immediately empowers you to create new conditions for a new way of life right here and now. Every moment is a potential moment of rebirth!

The past does serve a very important purpose. It gives you a breadth of knowledge and experience regarding action and reaction and how certain thoughts and behaviors result in certain consequences. Memory provides a very important basis for new choices. This history of awareness regarding how the world has worked and the memory of what your previous thoughts and feelings produced are priceless because they relate to what you intend for your life right now.

Those individuals who are the most honest with themselves and the most unafraid to look at their past and what they have created up until this point—free from shame, guilt, and regret—are blessed with the greatest power to collapse time and manifest what they desire. They are most willing to gain new insight and learn. **Those who have not been able to admit responsibility or acknowledge that previous choices did not serve them or others will remain stuck in time and burdened with the pain and karma that come with this state of ignorance.**

Mastering your reality requires you to operate your life with a greater sense of presence. **Conscious creation can only happen in**

the present moment. Understanding this is a huge step to becoming more present every day. As it has been said before, "Trying to drive a car by looking in the rearview mirror will only get you in an accident." To be a powerful creator, you must see the past for the perfection of the way it unfolded, take what valuable information you can from it, and apply what you learned along the way.

THE POWER
OF FORGIVENESS

Any negative thought or unsettling belief you hold in your mind has energy associated with it that adds weight to your spirit and acts as a drag on time. This includes thoughts about anyone in your life whom you blame or hold in contempt for things that have happened in your past. Holding a grudge is like poison to the mind of someone who desires the most joyful and fulfilling life possible. Every last resentment and call of "foul" must be rooted out of your mind in order for you to speed up the journey to creative and spiritual liberation.

Since you were young, you may have been holding others accountable for your circumstance in life. This could be anyone from a mother, father, sister, brother, aunt, uncle, friends, teachers, religious leaders, ex-wife or husband, business partner, girlfriend, or boyfriend. Somebody did something to you that caused problems and made you say, "I cannot and will not ever forgive them."

We hear about forgiveness a lot, especially as it relates to self-help and personal healing. We are often told that the only one we are really hurting through contempt and anger toward others is ourselves. While it is true that holding on to this negative energy predominantly affects you and your precious and powerful state of mind, it also has a profound effect on everyone around you. **Even more important, a negative state of mind has a significant effect on how things unfold for you in your next moments.** I want to go a bit deeper here and show you how the mind-set of contempt and blame really works at a fundamental level on your ability to create.

At the heart of blame, contempt, vengeance, and condemnation is resistance. This resistance is completely understandable given the fact that for many victims, the hurt, pain, and anger may have been extremely severe. Physical, sexual, verbal, and mental abuse, along with many other extremely painful experiences, can cause people to feel like they cannot forgive their abusers. This resistance and anger is how the mind has worked to protect itself if these painful experiences ever happen again.

A major survival instinct we all have is the ability to recognize patterns in our world. This helps us categorize and deal with a host of life situations, especially those that may be threatening. When we experience something painful, we make it a priority to detect similar situations to ensure as much as possible that we won't suffer in the same way again. Categorizing someone in our mind as a threat after they hurt us in some way is a prime example of this. Having anger and contempt for a person who has wronged us works as a form of protection and prevention. This state of mind, however, is not helpful to you in terms of becoming the most powerful creator you can be. One, it can cloud your vision in a way where you see or feel threats in your world where they don't exist, and two, this negative attitude itself is an energy drain that limits you in some way from being in the most liberating and creative state of mind possible.

Here's why: Holding resistance toward any part of your past is like saying that it had no purpose. It is, in a sense, a form of resistance to the perfection of the universe, and even more specifically, it is a demonstration of resistance to a part of your perfection. In no way, shape, or form am I saying that the wrongs you experienced were acceptable actions. **Forgiving or accepting the past behavior of another is not condoning their behavior in any way.** It does not mean you have to engage with this person again. It does not mean you don't need to take precautions with them. It is acknowledging what has happened, and it is demonstrating faith that there was and is a specific reason why it happened for you on your personal journey.

Things never happen to you—they happen *for* you.

Now, some may read this and wonder about all the horrors going on in the world and say, "Really? All of this is happening for a reason? Tell that to the parent of a lost or sick loved one." No one can know the sacred purpose for any experience that another person has gone through. What you can be assured of is that if you witnessed a horrible act happen to another person or something terrible has happened to you at some point, there is a reason for it as it relates to your journey of understanding and awareness. Every part of reality, including the more challenging ones, offers you a new way of looking at the dynamic and deep connection between you and life. A new possibility of who you are is asking to be accepted.

How you decide to interpret your life thus far is everything as it relates to what unfolds next. Holding on to a negative experience and denying that there was a purpose to it demonstrates a lack of faith in a universe that has birthed you into existence and provided you with everything you have needed to be here, in this moment, right now.

Your story has tremendous value to your world. The more you can embrace the idea that there is a divine reason why your path has unfolded in the way it has, the more trust you will have in your world, and the more impact you will have. This does not mean you ignorantly put yourself in harm's way or need to interact with the people who caused you pain. But it does mean that you can look at their participation in your life in a new way. Maybe the painful experience set you on a path to life's answers at a much more accelerated pace than would have been possible had that event not happened. Maybe you learned how strong you really are. Maybe it has shown you that there isn't anything you can't overcome in your life. You may become a great light and a wonderful, hopeful example to millions of people. You may already be this example as a result of the challenges you've overcome just to be in this very moment, reading these words.

This is not about accepting that something had to happen to you; it is about acknowledging that it *did* happen and standing in front of the universe saying, "I trust that there is perfection and a specific, divine purpose for my past and the exact way it unfolded.

Because of this, I am realizing more of my unlimited potential for the future."

This is a very powerful state of mind!

WHEN YOU CAN LOOK AT life this way, there is nobody to hold in contempt for anything, because it was all vitally important to your growth and development. **Your universe is seen as a field of possibility where it is not about what has happened, but rather who you decide to be in this moment with what is happening.** This frees you from resisting any part of the past, bringing you into this powerful moment and the amazing new possibilities that await you!

EMBRACING YOUR PERFECTION

Forgiveness and the ending of resistance is not just about your past and the others who you felt wronged you. Most important, it is about you. Releasing yourself from any thoughts of guilt, shame, and regret is mind-blowingly powerful as it relates to the creation of everything you desire. The larger implications for your life are astounding when you can see yourself free from any negative label of your past. Once again, this is not about ignoring responsibility or karma from past actions. It is simply about shedding the damaging labels you've held in your mind that do not serve you any longer. What this process is really leading you to is the reality of your perfection; your *absolute* and *complete* perfection.

If you can see a perfect past for yourself, you can see a perfect present.

We have been so conditioned, generation after generation, to see our flaws and our imperfections, that we have become obsessed with being accepted and loved, chasing a vision of unattainable perfection. Pop culture floods us with images of what it takes to be perfect, look perfect, and act perfect. We are bombarded on TV, in magazines, and other media with stories about people who have millions of dollars. We are barraged with images of what the perfect body, weight, hair, or face should be. We are constantly trying to measure up to some illusion of what perfect looks like, what possessions perfect has, and what perfect acts like.

Being endlessly confronted with images like this, one can easily lose perspective. It becomes almost commonplace to get down on yourself and feel incomplete or inadequate. Herein lies the very heart of the creation of an undesired reality. There is no bigger way to limit your creative power and extend time than a self-deprecating mind-set.

It was this one single realization of the truth of personal perfection that led to my massive breakthrough. An amazing mental and spiritual liberation ensued. This one understanding caused the dam of truth to burst and self-love flowed freely and fully. I had been so hard on myself for so long that I had no idea how much baggage I was carrying as it related to self-loathing and a sense of incompleteness. Letting go of any sense of regret, guilt, or shame was what opened the door to a whole new thought process on what is possible. Self-love covered every corner of my mind and body as I realized that the sense of personal perfection or completeness, which had seemed elusive to me for so many years, already existed in this moment! A new beautiful and grace-filled understanding took hold. I AM That. The world never looked the same again.

The following examples are used to show you how all the dots connect from mind to thought to feeling to action. As you read them, it becomes easy to see how guilt, shame, and regret work against you and your dreams.

If you feel guilty about your past, then in some part of your mind, there is a truth you hold that says, "I AM guilty." If you hold regret at some level of your identity, there is a truth you hold that says, "I AM regretful." And of course, if you feel shameful for something you did five, ten, or twenty years ago, there is still a truth embedded in your core identity (I AM) that says, "I AM shameful."

As mentioned earlier, the way life works is that thought must become reality, mind must become matter, "I" must become "AM." These truths that you hold in your subconscious will eventually need to be experienced as real again. Therefore, the ego, as directed by the beliefs you hold, will work to make sure that these beliefs can be validated. The ego will drive you to make the exact choices needed to put the right people, places, and events together in order for you to feel the truth of shame again. Your ego will ensure that you make the exact choices necessary to feel extremely regretful about something else in your life. Your ego, as the extremely loyal protector, defender, and creator of what you believe to be true about yourself, will cause you to do something that makes you feel guilty all over again. All of this is the perfect and elegant design of the universe to support you and your truth.

These examples indicate how imperative it is on the path of

personal empowerment to see the beauty and serendipity of your past and present perfection. This is what you want the ego to honor! It does not matter what happened to you as a child. It does not matter if you were abandoned, put up for adoption, abused, called dumb or worthless, never hugged, or if you had emotionally unavailable parents, never knew your parents, or any of the thousands of other possible negative scenarios. **None of these experiences ever once affected your ABSOLUTE PERFECTION. You are as perfect in this moment as you have been since the day you were born.**

WHEN WE ARE CHILDREN we tend to interpret any acts that cause us mental anguish as signs that something is wrong with us, rather than see any wrong with the people who have actually maligned us. We turn these events into the belief that we are unworthy in some way that has caused these unpleasant things to occur.

Nothing could be further from the truth; however, our identity during these young, formative years is very naive and impressionable. Painful childhood experiences and the way we interpret them get embedded deep into our psyche. As a result, our life's path and the choices we make become the evidence of this misunderstood identity. As the mental anguish from these choices continues, questions are continually being asked regarding, "Why?"

The interesting thing about the universe is that it is always listening and responding. When the pain of a life of suffering becomes intolerable, a prayer, a cry, a wish, or a genuine yearning for clarity and answers will be expressed. When the "time" is right, meaning when you are ready to receive the necessary information for change, these answers will reveal themselves. This happens on an array of different issues and at a host of different times in our lives. Can you see it even right now in these words in front of you?

This reminds me of a powerful story from my childhood. When I was growing up, my father always amazed me with how handy and smart he was. Anything that needed to be built, repaired, taken apart, or put back together he could do it. He fixed almost everything that broke in our house. He fixed our cars and the neighbors' cars when they broke down, and he refinished our entire basement, electrical and all. He even had a side hobby of building transistor radios from scratch. I was continually enamored with what he could do. Being that I was very curious, I wanted to learn everything I could from him so on many occasions I would sit with him while he worked on our house or took apart the engine of our car. I wanted to be around him and I was trying to soak up as much information as I could. Often I would ask if I could help. He would sometimes let me, but reluctantly. What would invariably happen is that I would eventually do something incorrectly and he would immediately let me know it. "That's all wrong. You don't know what you are doing," he would say. Or "Don't be so stupid," or even, "You're doing that like an idiot."

I remember my mother hearing this on different occasions from inside the house and yelling out to the garage, saying, "Stop talking to him like that!" Over time I started to get very bothered by his disapproval and what seemed like my inability to do anything right in his eyes. Eventually I became very upset and negatively affected by his words. I desperately wanted my father to approve of me and I knew I could learn how to do these things well. "What is wrong with me?" I often wondered.

One evening, when I was about thirteen years old, I was in our family room watching TV while my parents and grandparents were sitting and talking in the kitchen. I immediately began to hear my father start in, "What are you talking about?" "Don't be so stupid." "That's all wrong." "You're acting like an idiot." *There he goes again*, I thought to myself. As I listened a bit closer and then actually leaned around the corner and looked in, however, I realized something startling. It wasn't my father I heard. It was my *grandfather* talking to my father!

In a flash, all of the anger I had held toward my father vanished. All of the contempt I held for him and for the way he spoke to me instantly turned to compassion. I now knew that the way he had been speaking to me was actually never about me, ever! It was all my father knew. This was how he had learned to communicate because this was how he was spoken to. Realizing this certainly didn't make it right, but it did explain his actions, and most important, it liberated me from any personalization of his criticism. This single yet profound realization released me from many of the negative feelings I previously had about myself. From that moment on, I was no longer affected by any condescension my father directed toward me. As an added benefit of this new understanding and my new peaceful responses, my father actually changed over time and eventually stopped speaking to me like his father spoke to him.

I want to be very clear here that my father and my grandfather were truly wonderful people in my life growing up. I am grateful for all of their love and support, and I have an incredible relationship with my father today. But like any learned, socialized behavior, it is passed from generation to generation; it is automatically regurgitated as if it is "normal" behavior. This happens until change is desired. Again, this does not excuse or in any way make acceptable the way I was spoken to at certain times in my life, or for that matter, the infliction of any kind of negative behavior on a child by a parent. But it does help in the reconciliation, understanding, and healing process for any individual who has suffered confusion and self-deprecation as a result of this type of interaction in their youth.

You define you. This is your greatest gift. No matter what anyone has ever said to you, told you, or done to you, it does not matter or have to be true for you anymore, from this moment forward. You hold the great power of self-definition, change, and time.

THE EVIDENCE OF THE PERFECTION of your past is simply that at each moment of your existence, you have chosen according to who you thought you were at the time. You chose based on what you felt you needed to do to survive in that particular moment in the environment you were in. Does this mean it was always "right" morally? No. Does this mean it was "right" based on what the law says? No. Does this mean it was always "right" based on the rules and judgments of religion and certain teachings of spirituality? No. Does this mean it was always "right" based on what you now believe? No. But for that time and that specific place in your life, it was exactly what you felt you needed to do, based on every ounce of accumulated knowledge and experience you had. Your past actions may not have been optimal; they may have had repercussions that you never want to repeat again, but they were still right in a way that is beyond reason. Your actions demonstrated the perfection of your identity at that time and even more important, they were part of the path of awareness that put you on the road to greater understanding and answers that you are on right now.

Again, accepting any of your past actions is in no way condoning them. It is liberating you to see that there is nothing in your past that should ever hold you back from your undeniable and absolute perfection right now. The truth is, you have never made a single mistake in your life. You may have had many "mis-takes" as it relates to creating what you desire in a shorter time frame, but every one of them occurred for a reason. Each of your experiences has been a learning experience.

The implications this has for you with regard to moving forward and collapsing time are dramatic. Any idea of imperfection will only serve to stretch time for you as it directly relates to what you really want. For example: If you see yourself as unlovable because of a childhood experience you had with your parents or because of a bad relationship, this identity will serve to keep the desire for true love as a desire rather than a reality. Your ego will keep you on a path to protect the belief that you are imperfect. When it comes to learning what you need to feel loved, your ego will keep this critical information away from you, so that you stay in relationships that make you feel unworthy of love.

To collapse time as it relates to your deep desire for true love, you must be willing to see your perfection. You must have the desire to love who you are and see love as a possibility for you. You must adopt this wholeheartedly as a new truth. The second you do this, your ego will go into overdrive, making new choices and sending out a new energy that begins to attract those who are looking for the same type of love. Your entire experience of "time" will change.

Life moves the exact information you've asked for into your reality on a constant basis. We only see and hear what we are ready to, however, when we are ready to. You could have told your best friend a hundred times that she needed to stop deluding herself about the guy she was dating so she wouldn't continue to get hurt. In the meantime, she stared back at you like she was looking right through you. Three weeks later, she may say, "I just met this wonderful new friend at yoga class, and we were having coffee when I told her about my relationship. She said I needed to wake up and see the truth of the situation now, so I can save myself from a whole lot of heartache in the future. Wasn't that kind? No one has ever been so direct with me."

It's probably a good thing that she can't see the steam coming out of your ears as you contemplate the one hundred or so times you patiently told her that very same thing. This is just more evidence demonstrating that everyone is on their own personal pace of "time" as it relates to what they want to know.

This reminds me of a woman I worked with, who was having trouble finding a man who would honor her and wasn't narcissistic and self-absorbed. On many occasions I offered that she must become what she was looking for in another person, or else she would attract a reflection of her own state of being in the next relationship. The universe was actually sending this message to her all the time through her suffering. She listened, but wasn't truly hearing the words yet.

Well, one night, I got a call from her, and she explained that she finally got it. She said, "I was at home this past Saturday night, feeling deeply lonely and sorry for myself. My mind raced—I felt like I was the only one in the entire world who was at home alone with no one to care about them or to love them. These feelings led into an all-out sobfest as I cried and cried about my situation and how hopeless I felt it to be. All of a sudden, after an exhausting time of this, I stood up from the curled ball that I'd been in on my bedroom floor, and in a fit of rage, I closed my eyes and screamed at the top of my lungs, 'I just want someone to love me!'

"When I opened my eyes, I was staring directly into my own reflection in the mirror hanging on my wall. It was as if I was frozen in a timeless moment of real understanding. The message became crystal clear. I needed to love, honor, and respect myself first before I could expect to receive it from anyone else."

JUST LIKE RELATIONSHIPS, if you are looking to flourish in your career, business, or with money in general, you must allow this experience into your present existence. Maybe when you were young, you grew up believing that you weren't worth having money, that it was not part of your family history, or that you weren't good enough or smart enough for it. If these beliefs were adopted into your identity, consciously or subconsciously, they may have had an effect on every decision you made regarding money. While these thoughts may have been believed as true in your past, they do not have to be true for your future.

The great news is that this is always a *new* moment. You are as capable of an abundance of success with money as anyone else. Is there a certain road and path to manifesting any new reality? Yes. You must understand and accept this. The first thing to do, however, is to wipe the slate clean as it relates to any negative or limiting thoughts. No matter what choices you have made that have kept you from success in the past, and no matter what your story has been in life, this is a new moment. Seeing yourself in a new way as it relates to having an abundance of money or thriving in your career will change every thought you have as to what is possible and how to create it. Your ego will honor the new truth of your value and worth, and you will begin to do things that you never even entertained doing before because your ego wouldn't allow it. You will make good decisions with money and make them with more confidence and ease.

What about right now? What new choices could you make now from a mind-set that sees a host of new possibilities for you?

If you are looking to be healthier or in better shape, you must hold an image of who you are at such a high level of acceptance and love that any other way of treating your physical body will become unacceptable. Before making this decision you may not have cared about what shape you were in or how healthy you were. With a new sense of honor and respect for yourself, the thoughts you have about eating certain foods will change. Every cell in your body will support this new truth. **Your appetite will completely change because your ego will no longer serve a poor self-image with a poor diet.** A new sense of self-appreciation will cause your ego to make exercise a priority. You will be energized and very focused on maintaining a healthy new diet. You will no longer resist this new identity; you will embrace it! Time will start to collapse, and before you know it, you will be a slimmer, more fit, and healthier version of who you are today.

These examples could go on as they relate to any other issue in your life. Each experience and every bit of pain you have felt as a result has been about nudging you to a greater understanding of who you are. At the core, pain is always a result of resistance to a greater sense of self-definition. The greater the belief in your imperfection and the idea that you are finite, the more you suffer and find ways to suffer. The miraculous journey of life and time is about discovering more and more of your limitless potential and magnificence!

> "Above all things reverence yourself."
>
> —PYTHAGORAS

LIFE WAITS FOR YOU TO claim more of your perfection so it can grace you with more. You will constantly be reminded of how much you believe this through your moment-to-moment state of mind. This is your litmus test. A disharmonious state of mind represents that for the moment you have forgotten this truth and in some way feel threatened or incomplete. The way out of this negative state is always found in taking a second to remember the truth—that despite everything you have been through in the past, you have overcome it all to be here right now. **In this moment, anything is possible.**

The ultimate truth is there has never been anything wrong

with you, there is nothing wrong with you, and there will never be anything wrong with you. You are a divine creation of a brilliantly elegant universe where every single thing in existence has a purpose and perfection. You are on a perfect journey to what you are destined to learn about the nature of who you really are. You are on your way to becoming more of a *master of your reality*.

OPENING TO
NEW POSSIBILITIES

What you are looking to create sits just beyond what you believe to be possible. The term *infinite possibility* is thrown around a lot in spiritual circles, but what it really means is that if you can embrace a universe that has no limits, and you are a part of this universe, then there should be no limits on what you believe is possible for your life.

Since we were young, our minds have been bombarded with notions of what can't be done or what we can't do or aren't good enough to accomplish. This has created a bubble of limits on possibility that is demonstrated in how we have created our lives. Opening to new possibility is about shattering the bubble of limits. It is about living in a space where the mind can open to new thoughts and actions.

Boundaries are necessary for our continued survival, and we are given them at a very young age. A key to becoming a powerful creator is to see that the boundary line of what is possible for you is not permanent but changeable and movable. It is movable by your desire, beliefs, and demonstrated will.

> **The moment you find the love to embrace a new possibility for yourself is the moment of conception that leads to the birth of a new reality.**

WHEN YOU ARE GROUNDED IN the present moment and more open to the perfection of who you are, the possibilities expand. This does not mean that you don't need to work tirelessly to put the necessary conditions together to achieve your dreams, but a huge step in this process is actually seeing what you desire as something that is possible, believable, and achievable.

Read each of the statements below. For the ones that are relevant to your desires, feel the truth of the statement deep within your mind. Read each statement until it feels comfortable, believable, and achievable. Read it until any resistance you feel toward what you are saying is completely gone.

- A lasting, intimate, passionate, loving relationship IS POSSIBLE FOR ME.
- A successful, exciting, enjoyable career path IS POSSIBLE FOR ME.
- A healthy, fit body IS POSSIBLE FOR ME.
- A financially secure life IS POSSIBLE FOR ME.
- A harmonious, peaceful relationship with my family IS POSSIBLE FOR ME.

- A loving, accepting, content relationship with myself IS POSSIBLE FOR ME.
- An empowered, exciting, and fulfilling way to know and experience life IS POSSIBLE FOR ME.

IF YOU CANNOT EMBRACE these truths, you are destined for a life in which you find yourself continually asking the question, "How do I change my situation?" Millions are plagued by events they don't understand, causing them to ask this question daily. What is interesting is that the universe's response to the "how" questions is often new challenges designed to get your attention. It is really about "when." As in *when* will you be ready for the answers? How much suffering do you need to go through until you submit to new information?

If your way of doing it worked, you wouldn't be asking the questions. By being willing to look at life in a different way, the answer to "how" magically surfaces. **Humility is the key to the door of wisdom.** The greater truth is that the universe has already answered you many times over. It is about finally being ready to open to the truth that is around you in this very moment, accepting it, and then putting the new awareness into action.

The reason why the truth of your perfection was emphasized earlier is that your personal identity is the key to TIME. The world can only respond to who you demonstrate you are and what you believe is true for you. Step one of collapsing time is seeing and believing in a new you and a new world of possibility for you.

If you believe yourself unworthy of deep, lasting love, but you say you want this type of love in your life, that disconnect will create time. It is not until you believe yourself worthy of this type of love that you will begin to attract it.

If you say you want a certain career, but remain completely oblivious to the arduous and dedicated path it takes to make the idea a reality, the disparity between your wishes and your awareness will create your experience of time.

If you are looking for spiritual wisdom, but avoid the self-reflection and true humility that this path requires, this resistance will be the source of the time it takes to experience the wisdom.

"Real knowledge is to know the extent of one's ignorance."

—Confucius

You cannot conceive of creating something you do not believe is possible. You can believe in something, but without the real desire for it to happen, you will never take the necessary steps toward creating it. And last, you can have a belief and desire, but without a will, you won't persevere through all the ups and downs required to see the dream become real.

The first key to speeding up time as it relates to your intention is to recognize when you lack the belief that what you desire is possible. The way to test this is to look at your actions and your current state of mind. Are you exactly where you desire to be right now? Do you have any fear about moving forward? Are you in the process of demonstrating that you truly believe in what you say you want for your life?

Intention + Personal Truth = Current Experience

THIS EQUATION REVEALS the creative nature of each human being. No matter who you are, by the example of your current circumstance and state of mind, you demonstrate what you have believed to be true. The most important question now is: What are you looking to experience as true from today forward?

HOW HARD YOU WORK TO create what you want is only limited by what you believe to be true for yourself. If you do not feel like you are getting any closer to what you want you will immediately ask questions and look for the answers, and that will help you. What is so incredibly amazing is that life will respond to you. It is responding in this very moment!

When you desire something specific, you draw in the knowledge needed to create it. You will also be confronted by endless examples of what you want that already exist and will encourage you to see that it is possible. Ever dream of a wonderful relationship and feel like you can't go anywhere without seeing happy couples living what seem like fairy-tale lives? It isn't happening to torture you, but to show you that it IS POSSIBLE, which also means if it is possible for them it is possible for you. It is those with a strong will to make things happen who can dream of and believe in things not yet known and make them a reality.

There are many larger examples from the history of mankind that demonstrate the power of believing in new possibilities and taking unrelenting action on them. This same power is in YOU. A couple of notable examples follow.

Martin Luther King Jr.'s vision and belief in the possibility of ending segregation and fighting for the civil rights of people of all races, colors, and religions sent him on an incredible and dramatic journey through demonstrations, speeches, and marches. This belief and will led to the Civil Rights Act, which was enacted July 2, 1964.

President John F. Kennedy's vision and belief in the possibility of putting the first man on the moon galvanized a whole nation as NASA sought to make this a reality. President Kennedy gave a speech declaring this intention on May 25, 1961. Just over eight years later, on July 20, 1969, American astronaut Neil Armstrong of the *Apollo 11* crew became the first man to step onto the surface of the moon. This incredible, world-changing event was completed in what seemed like lightning speed based on the enormity of the intended goal.

> "Don't tell me the sky's the limit when there are footprints on the moon."
>
> —Paul Brandt

. . .

IN A MORE CONTEMPORARY CONTEXT, we see this belief with athletes who had dreams, like LeBron James, Jackie Joyner-Kersee, or Michael Phelps. We see it with actors and actresses who, upon winning an Academy Award, say, "Ever since I was little, I dreamed of this moment." We see it with entrepreneurs who say, "I had the vision that this product or service would one day become a reality." We see it with many people who dream big and go far.

In one of his Nike ads, Michael Jordan made an incredibly powerful and insightful statement that epitomizes the transcendent power of intention. This intention carried him through the many days of hard workouts and heartbreaking playoff losses that were part of his journey to six NBA championships with the Chicago Bulls. Jordan said:

"I have something more important than courage—I have patience. I will become what I know that I AM."

When your belief reaches this pinnacle level and you combine it with an unwavering faith in the completion of your desire, time is no longer a factor. You are not focused on the question "When?" but rather on the more creative, faith-filled path of "How?" When you are so involved in the "how," your dream seemingly becomes real in no time. There is no resistance to the process or the possibilities because you are only focused on what is possible, rather than on what is not possible.

This reminds me of a story related to how fast the universe responds to the truth you hold about any situation you face. It is an example of the remarkable power we have in relation to the creation or collapse of time and circumstance. Although this example may seem minute, the implications for change in your life based on a new mind-set are enormous.

IN 2006, my family and I were on a winter trip with three other families that are very good friends of ours. After a long and tiring, but very fun, day spent skiing and sledding, everyone was hungry for a big dinner. We decided to order out. One of the other fathers and I drove about fifteen minutes into town to pick up the food. When we came out of the store and got in the car to go home, we saw that the road was completely congested with traffic as far as the eye could see. The road, a two-lane highway, was entirely backed up in both directions. It appeared that we were going to be delayed for a long time. My friend instantly became agitated and his whole demeanor changed. There was so much traffic backed up that he didn't even think we'd be able to get out of the parking lot. Immediately the negative statements started coming out of his mouth. "Oh, this is great; we will never get home," "It's going to be hours," and "Dinner will be ruined!"

Upon hearing this, I took the opportunity to present a new way he might want to consider dealing with the situation. I told him that there were many other possibilities that could unfold. I also explained how his beliefs and negative energy were contributing to the situation. He looked at me suspiciously, but asked curiously, "How in the world am I part of the reason this is happening?" Without going into much detail, I told him that since everything is energy, his resistance was part of the force that was keeping the unwanted reality in place. If he wanted to get home with the food sooner, resisting what was happening was not the best energy to put toward the circumstance. He then said half sarcastically, "OK, what am I supposed to do—just say I couldn't care less how long this traffic issue lasts? And I couldn't care less if someone even lets me out of this parking lot or not?" My response was, "Exactly. Let it all go. Also, ask yourself what benefit the negative energy is to your situation. Why not try it? Take a deep breath, accept the truth that is before you for the moment, open to all the other possibilities, and let go of all expectation. What do you really have to lose, anyway?" This last statement seemed to shift something in him. He stared at me for a long moment, as the truth of what was offered seemed to settle into his mind at a very deep level. He looked back out the window, stared into space, and with a true sincerity said, "OK, I release it all and I accept it all."

As if on cue, at that very instant, a gentleman in a car in line on the highway rolled down his foggy, iced-up window, stuck his hand out of the car, and actually waved us out of the parking lot.

After a long moment of staring blankly at the man in sheer shock, as if saying to himself, "Is he really talking to me?" my friend snapped out of it, quickly took his foot off the brake, and drove into the opening that this very kind driver had created for us in the line of traffic. Within a minute or two, traffic freed up and we were on our way home. My friend's initial fears never materialized. Something much more profound occurred. This one powerful moment ended up changing the way he now looks at the entire way he deals with life. A completely new understanding of how the energy of his thoughts affects his reality and the possibilities within it was revealed.

Small, everyday examples like this show how the simple energy of a new thought can immediately change your circumstances and the experience of time. The key is to become more and more aware of when you are adding to the amount of time it takes to create what you want through the resistance of limiting thoughts, rather than sending out a powerful energy of possibility and belief that works to dissolve the undesired conditions.

No matter what you believe for the moment, the universe will be here to help support you based on these beliefs. What a wonderful thing to realize! If one can literally change the experience of traffic with a single change in energy and belief, imagine what else is possible!

The universe has always been there for you, but now you are on the path to learning exactly *how* it supports you in your every moment of thought and being.

EVERY THOUGHT, FEELING, AND ACTION you have are producing an energy that is impacting the circumstances all around you. This is how vital an ever-expanding consciousness is to the quality of your life. You are learning how powerful you truly are, how much you matter, and how you can choose to immediately impact your situation and your world. A lifetime of endless new possibilities awaits!

THE PROCESS
OF POWERFULLY
CREATING YOUR LIFE

> "Mastering others is strength. Mastering yourself is true power."
>
> —LAO TZU

Mastery over life emerges from a deep understanding of and mastery over *oneself*. Without embracing more of the notion of personal perfection and love, what the world offers you will be limited in some way. If you are looking to be in the most powerful state of mastering time and how things get created for you, it is imperative that you reflect on your thoughts and make sure that you have no doubts about what you want and what you are worthy of accomplishing.

This transformational process of condensing time and mastering creation is for those ready to embrace all that life has to offer. The process is for those who are unafraid of failure and for those who are willing to learn from as many failures as it takes to get it right. It is for those who are open to all the possibilities.

The key components of creation—*belief, desire, will,* and *faith*—are all based on the degree of appreciation, respect, and love you have for yourself. Without self-love, there is a big risk that your creative process will be dominated by an ego that needs to demonstrate a lack of this love. You remain frustrated and feel unfulfilled in certain ways. This will occur regardless of how many journals or vision boards you put together.

Any lack of total self-acceptance and self-love will impact your choices in a way that will keep you stuck in the story of "why" and "when" rather than the reality and true power of "now" and "how."

A loving and peaceful vision of who you are does not guarantee that everything you desire will manifest itself for you on cue. You still have to really want to create your intent. You still have to work at it every day. Like they say in some religious circles, "You can pray, but you still have to shuffle your feet." What self-acceptance does for you is clear the path of ignorance, self-sabotage, and delay. It gives you a balanced state of mind that leads to clearer choices each day. There is nothing more powerful and time-dissolving than inner confidence and knowledge that allows you to transcend all doubt.

THE AMAZING STORY of swimmer Diana Nyad offers a wonderful recent example of the power of belief, intention, and an unrelenting will to overcome all obstacles and doubt.

Born on August 25, 1949, Diana began her career as a world-class swimmer in her mid-teens. As a young girl, she dreamed of competing in the 1968 summer Olympics, but in 1966 she contracted an infection of the heart that caused her to be laid up in bed for three months. By the time she got well, she had lost some speed in her swimming, and her Olympic opportunity passed.

In college, Diana gravitated to marathon swimming and set a women's world record in her first race, a ten-mile swim in Lake Ontario in 1970 that she completed in four hours and twenty-two minutes. Throughout the 1970s, Diana achieved numerous accomplishments for distance swimming including, at age twenty-six, swimming around the entire island of Manhattan in just under eight hours. In her last competitive race in 1979, on her thirtieth birthday, she set a world record for distance swimming—going an incredible 102 miles from Bimini Island in the Bahamas to Juno Beach, Florida, in 27.5 hours. Her biggest accomplishment was yet to come, however, and proved to test her will to an incredible degree.

Since Diana's mid-twenties, it had been a huge goal for her to be the first person to swim straight through from Cuba to Florida without a protective shark cage. She made her first attempt to swim from Havana, Cuba, to Key West, Florida, in 1978 at age twenty-eight. During this attempt, she was able to cover about seventy-six miles before strong winds pushed her off course and ended her swim.

Even though it had been more than three decades since her first attempt, in 2010, at the remarkable age of sixty, Diana became determined to make this goal a reality and began training for her next attempt at this record. Her second try at this milestone occurred on August 7, 2011, almost thirty-three years after her first. This time her swim was stopped some twenty-nine hours later after strong winds, shoulder pain, and a bout of asthma prevented her from finishing.

Her third attempt was undertaken on September 23, 2011, but came to an end forty-one hours and sixty-seven nautical miles into the journey due to jellyfish and Portuguese man-of-war stings.

Undeterred, her fourth attempt occurred on August 18, 2012. This time the swim was ended because of bad weather as Diana encountered two major storms during her swim. She also incurred nine jellyfish stings. She did cover more miles in this swim than on any of her previous three attempts.

On the morning of August 31, 2013, Diana Nyad set out on her fifth attempt at being the first person to swim nonstop from Havana, Cuba, to Florida. The distance was 110 miles. On September 2, 2013, at 1:55 p.m. Eastern Standard Time, fifty-three hours after she started her swim and thirty-six years after she started her journey, sixty-four-year-old Diana Nyad stepped onto the beach in Key West, Florida. The dream had finally been realized.

Diana's story of perseverance is an extraordinary example of the power of intention and will to achieve a dream regardless of the obstacles or number of previous unsuccessful attempts. Diana Nyad mastered time by never letting her age or the time it took to accomplish her dream become a negative factor in her outlook or drive. The power of unlimited belief, self-respect, and love are all on wonderful display through Diana's personal and athletic journey to this amazing accomplishment.

We all have the free will to determine how we are going to look at our circumstance in life. Each of us has the ability to determine what is possible in this moment, regardless of what has happened in the past. There is not a single person in the world who is not worthy of unrestricted self-love and the freedom and peace of mind it brings. This state of respect and honor is the key to all creative energy. Every human being in every moment is worthy. No one is denied who allows for this grace. The universal response to this love is unconditional and everlasting.

The Creative Process

STEP 1: SETTING INTENTION

Setting a powerful intention requires that you get very focused on the deepest desires of your heart. Start from the vision that feels the best when you picture it. The idea is to get the very clearest image you can get of what you want to create for yourself. If you can't see it clearly yet, this is OK. The point is to set your mind on something as close as possible to what you want. Your good and bad experiences along the way will help shape this vision into one that becomes clearer and more fine-tuned.

What is currently in your life is a result of all that you have believed and focused on as real and achievable prior to this moment. It is the result of a life of experiences and lessons, mistakes and feedback. Everything you've been through has worked on a subconscious level to expand your awareness and sharpen the vision of what you want. The process is the same when you work from a conscious level to actively create what you desire. The difference is that at a more conscious level, you are able to see the signs quicker, gain valuable information faster, and make new helpful choices much sooner than you did before.

. . .

A MIND THAT IS OPEN to what is possible is a key to the power behind your intention. Working from a belief in unlimited potential for yourself is like swimming with the flow, while working from a sense of limited possibility makes your efforts feel like you are swimming against the current. When you really believe in and feel worthy of new possibility for yourself, no part of your identity or ego works against this intention or tries to slow it down. Therefore, it manifests for you much quicker. There is no part of you that is subconsciously trying to prove yourself wrong. There are no brakes on your manifesting power!

New Year's resolutions provide an interesting example of how this works. Often these resolutions are focused on behavior, such as getting up earlier, working out more, eating less, planning better, etc. Usually, many of these resolutions are already broken or forgotten about two weeks to a month into the new year. **The reason is this: In order for your behavior to change, your feelings must change. For your feelings to change, your thoughts must change. And for your thoughts to change, the perception of who you are (I AM) must change.** Working to change only your actions generally will not work, which is why many New Year's resolutions don't make it past January. The real power of change is in the work of redefining who you are.

The next chart represents the flow of life. Working against this flow can be draining and frustrating. However, working from the source of your thoughts, feelings, and actions, or with the flow, is both empowering and liberating.

The Flow of Life

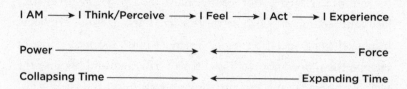

THE FLOW IN LIFE HAPPENS when who you are (I AM) is aligned with the corresponding thoughts, feelings, and actions (movement from left to right). Otherwise it will feel like you have to use a lot of force to make changes. For example, if who you are is not totally engaged in the benefit of being physically fit, it will seem like a lot of work to get up early in the morning and go to the gym. If who you are is not free from the idea that you can survive without your addiction, it will seem very hard to stop using drugs when you get the urge. If you are someone who is used to drama and anxiety as a part of each day, it will feel uncomfortable to be relaxed and worry-free for long periods of time.

Trying to force actions and behaviors that are in conflict with who you truly believe you are is energy-draining and tiring to the soul. It doesn't matter who you "think" you are, the truth of who you "believe" you are is always self-evident by your current actions or resistance to new choices and actions. Moving from right to left in the chart above is what causes time to stretch as it relates to carrying out the changes you desire. Trying to act against your true identity is the way of force, and the one thing force produces is counterforce. **Real personal power is found when you work from left to right, from a change in I AM to a change in action.**

Trying to change your actions alone is an uphill battle because for actions to change, your feelings must change. Trying to change just your feelings can also be very tiring. These feelings are being produced for a specific reason. Trying to just suppress them or change them does not work and feels very unnatural because the negative energy that is moving through your mind and body is real and is looking for an outlet. To dissolve the negative energy and change your feelings, you must understand the thoughts that are causing them. Trying to just change your thoughts can also seem like a lot of work. The reason for this is that these thoughts are being supported by some idea you have about life. There is a specific reason you believe and perceive things the way you do. Your thoughts are supporting your truth. **These negative thoughts will only change when you have truly redefined who you are (I AM).**

The origin of all the energy you put toward what you create for yourself comes from your I AM statements. This is where the ability to make real changes comes from, how you get in the flow, and how you collapse time. This is precisely why a good part of this book is dedicated to opening your mind to bigger possibilities for yourself. **It is about nudging you to the truth that who you really are is more magnificent than you have ever even remotely imagined. This is what changes the experience of "time" for you and where more of your full creative potential is released. Flow, serendipity, and synchronicity then become experiential and commonplace.**

The power of setting intention and believing in accomplishing this vision cannot be underestimated. It is the defining X factor affecting how and when any dream or idea comes together for you.

MY BROTHER GARY'S JOURNEY TO finding his career and passion is a very inspiring example of the power of following one's heart with a faith that transcends all fear. Gary is five years younger than I am, and after graduating from college, he decided to do as I did and began working in finance. This served him well for a time, but he wasn't sure whether finance was his calling or whether it was how he wanted to spend the rest of his life. But given that he was only in his mid-twenties at the time, it was as good a place as any to start out and get some experience in the working world.

As he reached his late twenties, my brother ran into some challenges that ultimately pushed him to question everything and begin to discover his real passion. After a few years, he found himself to be less and less fulfilled working in the financial business. During that time, he and his girlfriend also broke off a very serious, long-term relationship. As a result, he became even more unhappy at work. He eventually came face-to-face with the truth that he didn't want to work in the financial business any longer. At thirty years old, he found himself in a position where he needed to sell his condo, change his outlook, and figure out what he really wanted to do with his life.

Over the next couple of years he explored several different jobs, including work in L.A. as a personal assistant to a major actor on a couple of movie sets. He didn't see this job moving in a direction that he truly desired either. So eventually he moved back to Arizona. He stayed in our spare bedroom for a few months as he tried to sort things out, do some soul-searching, and find the right direction for his life.

For many months he struggled with finding clarity until the moment came when the time was right for change. One day, after we had a long talk, I was very direct with him and said, "What is it that you truly want to do with your life?" He looked up at me, and with a knowing and certainty I'll never forget, he said, "I want to live in New York and work in the fashion industry." Well, as you might imagine, I was a bit surprised and responded, "Well, that's great, but you can't just head for New York without any money or experience and simply enter the fashion industry. How do you plan on financing a huge move like this?"

"I'm going to sell my car," he said. I was shocked. His car was all he had left to his name. He had sold his condo a couple of years earlier, hadn't worked since he came back from L.A., and was almost completely out of money. His 1995 Volkswagen Jetta was the last remaining asset he had.

"How much do you think that will get you?" I asked.

"About five grand," he responded.

I quickly calculated that that amount would be enough for one month in New York, at best. "Are you sure? What if this plan doesn't work?" I said.

"It will," he responded quickly and emphatically.

I didn't know what to say. Every part of me wanted to believe that what he was saying would actually happen, but I couldn't help but think about what he would do if it didn't work out. What's interesting is that my feelings didn't matter one single bit. It was all about his level of determination and belief. At that critical moment, the most important thing was that he was finally certain.

Two weeks later, he sold his car, and with $5,500 cash in his pocket, he moved to his friend's apartment in New York, where he was invited to stay for at least a month. It was as though he were part of a movie cliché—moving to the Big Apple to make his dream come true.

As soon as he got there, he started working with a job placement agency. Three weeks later, he had already had four job interviews. A couple of them were for positions as an assistant to top executives at some very big companies. I spoke to him just after he received his third job offer. I was so incredibly happy for him.

"Which one are you going to take?" I asked him in a sort of astonished state.

His response nearly stopped my heart. "None of them." he said. "I've already turned the first two down, and I'm about to tell the third one, 'Thanks, but no thanks.'"

Silence. I was stunned. So many thoughts flashed through my mind that I almost couldn't get the words out. Three weeks into his journey, almost all his money gone, and here he was, turning down three—count them, three—job offers with big, influential businesspeople in one of the biggest cities in the world.

"Are you insane?" I asked.

Calmly and clearly he said, "I am holding out for the one I really want. My fourth interview is for an assistant job with the head creative director of one of the biggest fashion brands in the world. However, I won't know whether I get the job until two days from now, and I need to respond to the offer I received from my last interview today."

This is the true meaning of faith: believing in something so much and being willing to risk everything for it, with no guarantee of success. This is the epitome of a powerfully creative way to go through life. It is a wonderful demonstration of will, belief, and the desire to follow your heart without any knowledge of the outcome.

As you can probably guess, he got the job. He worked successfully in New York with the brand for several years until they moved him back out to L.A. Now, eight years later, he is still in the industry doing what he loves to do every single day.

WHEN MY BROTHER MADE THAT important decision on my couch some years ago, he did it with such a certainty, focus, and demonstrable faith that the universe had to take note. Millions of unseen lines of connection between him and his world were severed in one instant and then reconnected in another, more fulfilling way in the next moment. They were reconnected with the right people who were drawn into his experience to play the necessary roles to make sure that his new belief and intended reality had a higher chance of coming together. He still had to follow through, show up every day, and work hard doing what he needed to do in the face of every challenge. But the ball was put in motion when my brother reached an *absolute* knowing of what he wanted, of what he was capable of doing, and of what he believed was possible for him.

Getting started on the vision you have for any aspect of your life is a critical first step toward demonstrating that you believe in yourself and in new possibilities. It is a start to the concept of collapsing time. Nothing you desire—whether it is in your relationships, family situation, job, financial issues, or personal outlook on life—should be off-limits.

It is interesting how it can seem easy to create something with very little effort in one area of your life, while in another area, it feels like climbing a steep mountain. More specifically, some people have no issue with manifesting money or a job, but cannot for the life of them keep a relationship in harmony for any extended period of time. Others have the greatest personalities and experience no problems with their family relationships, friendships, or romantic partners; however, ask them why they are having so much trouble with their finances or money, and it's a head-scratcher. They either don't know why, or have a chain of excuses for why things haven't worked out.

Often problems in different areas of life are all connected but as in the examples before, a person can see and believe in what they want with total certainty in one area of life, but in another, they don't have a shred of self-acceptance or belief that they are worthy of it.

Accomplishing or creating something for yourself is not a matter of time; it is a matter of consistent demonstrated intention.

ANOTHER EXAMPLE OF THE POWER of intention is ironically about my other sibling, my sister, Tracy. Tracy is the middle child and the only girl, stuck right between Gary and myself. She has always had a determined will; with an older and a younger brother, she learned to be strong and stand up for herself at a very young age. This strength has been helpful to her in many important ways over the course of her life.

I first learned about her career aspirations on the day she graduated from college. I was helping her move out of her apartment, when we started talking about what she was going to do now that she was out of college. Her response took me a bit by surprise. "Well, I'm moving to L.A., and I'm going to make it in the movie business," she said resolutely.

I was confused. "As an actress?" I said.

"No," she responded. "I want to create and produce."

I was a bit stunned. I had never known that this was what my sister wanted to do; yet what struck me was that it was such a specific intent. She seemed like she had been thinking about it for quite a long time.

"I have a friend I'm going to room with out there while I look for a job," she explained. And with that, a week or so after graduation, she was off to L.A. to follow her passion and her dream.

There is no substitute for a strong will and a laser-focused intent. One of the great benefits of having a will this concentrated is the energy it brings with it that draws in and lines up all the necessary conditions and synchronicities. This includes all the so-called fortunate breaks that occur that help you on the path to your desires. When you are going through the process, it can be difficult at times to see how all these lines connect or why some periods of silence or suffering are necessary. Yet it all has a place in leading to what you truly desire to create.

Within a week of moving to L.A., my sister had a temp job as an agent's assistant at the largest talent agency in the world. Cutting her teeth there, she worked her way up for several years, going from being this particular agent's third assistant to his head assistant. All the while, she barely had enough money to live on. On top of that, she was logging very long hours, which made it impossible to have any social life whatsoever. I remember many nights when I would call her at eight, nine, or ten o'clock, and she would still be in the office working away. Often this was on a Friday or Saturday night.

This period had its rewards. Ultimately she became so highly respected for how hard she worked and how well she handled herself in her job that she was asked to enter the exclusive agents program and become an agent for the firm. This was a huge opportunity. Of the thousands of résumés that a firm like this takes in, only a very few get this chance. Remaining true to her passion to create rather than to manage people, she declined the offer (a bold move in itself) and left to take a position heading development for a small film company in New York. Still barely getting by and working incredibly long hours, she helped find quality scripts and make several major movies. One of the beautiful scripts she was responsible for finding and developing, *A Lesson Before Dying* from HBO Films, received an Emmy for best screenplay and the Emmy for Best Picture. Eventually she moved back to L.A. to work for another film company and added to her reputation of being able to find great material to develop and produce.

In 2005, just a little over twelve years after graduating college with a dream to make movies, my sister took a major chance and left her secure job at her well-funded film company to produce on her own. She made the move because she had found a script that she firmly believed was worth taking a chance on making. This was a huge risk. She had no guarantee that anything would happen with the film. She faced the possibility of being jobless and having major financial problems if it didn't come together. This was all done on pure faith.

As providence would have it, not one, not two, but three of the biggest names in the movie industry signed on to do the movie: Robert Redford, Meryl Streep, and Tom Cruise. Not bad for her first solo producing job.

The film, *Lions for Lambs*, tells a poignant story about the politics of war and the impact and responsibility every citizen has toward their country and the world. The film's message about the difference we can each make through our everyday choices is just as relevant today as when it was made.

After her work on this film, she was hired as an executive VP of production for one of the biggest film companies in the world, and today, she continues to produce major motion pictures. At her relatively young age, Tracy has worked with an incredible list of actors, actresses, directors, and producers that are household names.

This entire journey of hers was rooted in a focused and intense desire and belief that was put into consistent, unwavering action for years. She stuck to her intention even through some very trying and painful times. There were many challenges and setbacks along the way. Yet her belief did not waver, no matter how far off-course life seemed to take her.

The point of all this is to demonstrate how life and "time" work with you when you are focused, certain in your beliefs, and in touch with your reality and how it works. My sister had virtually no money when she went out to L.A. She also had no major connections in the film business when she left Arizona to follow her path. When she was struggling to find the right opportunities in between jobs for months at a time, she had to humble herself and live with friends. She also had the added pressure of working her way through the ranks of the film business as a woman in what has been a very male-dominated industry. This was both frustrating and exhausting to deal with at times. Nonetheless, she consistently stayed steadfast in her belief in herself and her ability to discover great material and do quality work as a producer in her field.

Time was not relevant to her in this process. What was relevant was moving forward each day, learning as much as she could and keeping her main goal in sight. When you operate from this mind-set, the universe and all the people and events around you conspire to help you put all the right conditions together. This is how life works! You and the way you put energy out manifest both the conditions and the people into your life to help you make your truth a reality.

This process works exactly the same for anything you want or desire. It could be about a better, more connected relationship; finding true love; feeling more at peace; changing your career; or getting into better shape. There is a path you must be willing to commit to and be ready to travel down. You must demonstrate what you believe to be true regarding who you are and what is possible for you through the eye of the toughest storms you encounter along your path.

You will be tested. There will be good times and bad times. Life is a school of learning and awareness that you cannot avoid on the way to your dreams or desires. **You must be confronted with what you need to learn along the way; this awareness may come through some very uncomfortable circumstances.** This is when your faith will truly be tested. When you do understand the bigger picture and submit to the process, however, time is truly on your side. The world becomes your oyster.

Great care needs to be taken to understand the following critical point. All things emanate from self-definition. There is no greater power to be realized than the power of I AM.

STEP 2: DECLARING I AM

To powerfully create, you must believe that you are capable of living the vision. It has to be part of who you know you are. This self-identity or these I AM statements are the driving factors of your life. It is where all the energy that goes into your daily choices and actions is sourced.

All things in existence are expressing their I AM by who and what they demonstrate themselves to be. To draw from an example in nature, an apple seed, unless genetically altered, will always grow into an apple tree. No matter how much you want the apple seed to become an orange tree, it matters not. It will express itself as the apple tree it is destined to become. A leopard, however, may seem like it's unable to change its spots, but if the terrain markedly changed color and shape, over generations the leopard would find a way to adapt or it would cease to exist.

As human beings, we have even more of a conscious, real-time evolutionary ability. We have the power of free will to redefine who we choose to be in any moment. This power should be great encouragement to any individual who has struggled. The discovery of this real-time power gives hope to humanity as a whole. Anyone with earnest desire can instantly change the energy they put out to their world. This "energy" is the key to what changes and what gets created.

The energy of I AM that comes out of you on a moment-to-moment basis is what is shaping your every experience in astonishing ways. Therefore, it is critical to conscious creation, collapsing time, and intentional manifestation that you become ever more aware of this driving force in your life.

Many times during our life, a change in self-identity or self-definition comes as a natural part of the maturation process. It becomes a normal learning curve as we go through the twists and turns of life. Other times, these changes are thrust upon us in startling and unavoidable circumstances or challenges. Examples include divorce, the passing of a loved one, a job loss, illness, etc. It is particularly important in these sudden, redefining situations to recognize the ability we have to choose how to interpret and react to our situation. It can mean the difference between realizing positive change over the course of a few weeks, or enduring a much longer period of suffering until we come to understand the purpose of what we faced.

A story that really epitomizes this idea is the life story of Dewey Bozella. Dewey Bozella was a young man who was trying to escape a rough upbringing and a challenging road in life when he was accused of murder in New York in 1983 at the age of twenty-three. The thing was, he didn't do it. A scared community and a de-

termined prosecutor, however, found a jury to convict him. Dewey
was sentenced on very little evidence to thirty years to life in prison
for a crime he steadfastly maintained he never committed.

Upon his incarceration, Dewey was faced with a choice. He
could be bitter and give up on life and the system for putting him
in the situation he was in, or he could accept where he was and
work from that point to change his life. It was after a few months
in jail that he made the critical decision to accept the circumstance, and use his time wisely and do the best he could to prove
his innocence over the coming years.

Dewey enrolled in the boxing program in New York's Sing-
Sing Prison and became a very skilled boxer. He eventually became the prison's light heavyweight champion. Through the
prison's educational program, Dewey got his bachelor's and master's degrees. He was a model prisoner and had sincerely adapted
to his circumstances, redefining his outlook and identity while
still working to clear his name and seek freedom.

In 1998, after fifteen years in prison, he got a break. Dewey
had contacted an organization called the Innocence Project about
his case. The Innocence Project is dedicated to helping those who
have been wrongfully imprisoned. After months and months of
writing to them, they finally looked at his case and then immediately got involved. After a thorough investigation, they discovered
that the prosecution in Dewey's case had deliberately left out critical DNA evidence that would have proven his innocence.

While the Innocence Project was working on his case, Dewey
had several opportunities to appear before the parole board. Each
time the parole board asked him for a confession, however, he refused. As he had maintained all along, he simply had not committed

the crime. At one point during his first retrial, he had the opportunity to be set free. The plea deal would grant him his freedom if he confessed to the crime. Again, staring straight into the face of freedom after having already spent twenty years in jail, Dewey chose to maintain the truth of his innocence rather than buckle to a prosecutor's pressure. This epitomizes the essence of true faith. Dewey's life as a free man hung in the balance; yet he demonstrated a strong self-respect, a trust in life and the power of the truth.

His second trial again ended in a guilty verdict. Dewey was devastated, but still refused to give up on his innocence or his day of ultimate justice. Eventually, the Innocence Project, together with a new law firm, got Dewey another trial based on evidence they discovered that had been held back and never presented at his original trial. This was a huge break. Finally, on October 8, 2009, after twenty-six years behind bars for a crime he never committed, Dewey was fully exonerated. He was finally a free man.

In July 2011, Dewey Bozella was presented with the Arthur Ashe award at the ESPYs (the ESPN sports awards show) for his boxing accomplishments in prison and overall courage and perseverance in the face of incredible adversity. It was a monumental moment for him after all he had been through. Dewey, however, wasn't done yet.

One of the big dreams he had when he was younger was to be a professional boxer. At age fifty-two, this dream was still very real to him even though others considered it a delusional fantasy. He realized his time had passed for a serious boxing career, but he still wanted just one professional fight.

There were many obstacles to overcome on this quest. No one over the age of fifty had ever been granted a license to box professionally in the United States. On Dewey's first attempt to pass a test that demonstrated he was fit to fight a sanctioned boxing association event, he was turned down. As you can probably guess, that didn't stop Dewey. He believed in himself regardless of time or age. It is truly magical what happens when you set your mind on something and have a faith that transcends all limits. Providence moves to serve you.

Providence in this case showed up in the form of Oscar De La Hoya, the six-time lightweight champion of the world, who had heard Dewey's story and was moved to help him achieve his goal. De La Hoya enlisted the help of a former world-class boxer to serve as Dewey's trainer to help prepare him to pass the licensing test. After working like he had never worked before to get in shape, Dewey passed the fitness test on his second attempt and became the oldest person ever to get a license to box in a sanctioned professional event.

On October 15, 2011, Dewey boxed against Larry Hopkins in his first and only professional fight—and won in a unanimous decision. It was a powerful and emotional moment for a man who had been on a long and trying road filled with many challenges, setbacks, and triumphs.

> "Don't give up, don't ever give up."
>
> —Jim Valvano

This true story epitomizes so many things about the nature of life, truth, faith, persistence, belief, and time. The way

Dewey handled what happened between his incarceration and his release determined everything. He knew who he was and he never wavered from his I AM statement (I AM innocent), regardless of who tried to make him say otherwise. He was willing to sacrifice one of life's most precious gifts, freedom, in order to maintain his innocence and self-respect. **Dewey decided not to let time be taken away from him, but rather, he embraced the truth of where he was and used time to his advantage to achieve what he had always dreamed.** This is truly a remarkable story of the human will and its relationship to life. Dewey's story was made into an inspiring documentary called *26 Years: The Dewey Bozella Story*, which was produced by ESPN films and released in 2012.

HEARING A STORY LIKE THIS can put so many things in our own lives in perspective. What challenges are you facing that give you the opportunity in this moment to redefine, declare, and demonstrate who you are? What I AM statements do you want to make about yourself that you can believe in and work to realize from this moment forward?

Life will work with you just like it always has. The power of choice that you have in this moment will determine your experience of time. How you answer the ultimate question of "Who am I?" is where your energy will flow from in every situation you face. It always has and it always will.

If Dewey Bozella had not stood firm in who he knew he was, he would have easily allowed others to shape his identity for him as a murderer. He would have allowed the state prosecutors, who never wanted to reveal that they had made a mistake, to have power over his life. He would have allowed the justice system to define him. Instead, at the cost of his own freedom, he persevered for himself and for all those whose lives have been affected by the same unfortunate circumstances in courts all over the world.

At the heart of the mechanics of how life comes together, there is a synchronicity and connectivity between everything in existence. All things in the universe are actually working together at the most subatomic level of existence to ensure the continuation of "life" and its perfection. It is the understanding of how this connection works that is the key to mastering life. It is the awareness of the relationship between you and all things in your reality and how they get arranged in each moment that opens the floodgates of personal power. This magical relationship is defined only by what you really believe to be true about who you are (I AM).

STEP #3: CULTIVATING
THE NECESSARY CONDITIONS

Life has a wonderful way of testing what you believe to be true: **action**. One of the requirements of conscious creation is that you participate in the process. Yes, inaction is also an option, but it may not produce the experience you are looking for. Inaction will eventually produce the awareness of what you need, but it is very unlikely to produce what you want.

Stating an intention and then declaring who you are in a way that aligns with your intention are two powerful parts of the manifestation process. Once you've done this, you cannot avoid the next step: demonstrating your will through your actions. What is interesting about this part of life is that you cannot fool the universe. You must not only act, but also act with the power of true belief behind the action.

Many people fool themselves into believing they are acting toward what they want in spite of the results. Going through the motions without real passion or belief, however, is a spiritually dead behavior. There is no creative power in this type of action. The offering in some circles of spirituality of the saying "ask, believe, receive" can be very misunderstood. Life only responds to the authentic truth you hold about yourself. This is the real creative energy that is getting released to your world every day.

Either you demonstrate yourself to be worthy or you do not. The identity deep down that says "I AM not worthy" will eventually produce a situation where life will make sure you know this to be true, as you get stopped cold on your career path, in your relationship, or in the attempt at any experience that would prove the opposite to you. This is one of the main reasons why the rap sheets of some criminals are so long. Many who preside over the justice system wonder why nothing changes in the behavior of those consistently punished. For many, it is like a revolving door back into prison. This is the perfection of life on full display. Personal identity is really what drives behavior, not the fear of punishment. If someone's identity is "I AM a criminal," it destines that person to consistently create that truth, unless the identity is changed. By validating our identities through our experience, we verify that we exist in the world. It is the self-fulfilling prophecy. If a prisoner, upon being released from jail still believes themselves to be a criminal, it will be a struggle to avoid the actions that once again define them as a criminal. Temptation, old survival habits, and the strong need to experience their identity will pull that person back toward the actions that previously defined them. This will be the case until a new identity is embraced.

Mastering time and building the foundation for an enriching life is an inside job first, not an outside one. The speed of your edification is determined by how authentic and honest you can be with yourself. You must come to understand who you have been and why you have demonstrated yourself in a certain way—without guilt, shame, or regret! This process reveals what has held you back. Becoming more conscious of how you have put the previous conditions of your life together is extremely valuable and a huge part of your spiritual journey through life. There are two powerful results from this process: one, you get to see what you created; and two, you get to see how you created it and how life has served your truth!

Let's return to the analogy of the seed. Every seed has an intention within it. There is a purpose and "seed" of possibility in this small kernel of matter. The potential of each seed is only part of the equation. What determines the result of how each particular seed ultimately expresses itself, how big it grows, how fruitful it becomes, and how long it takes to fully mature depend on how the seed is nurtured.

Many conditions need to come together for a particular seed to become what it intends to become. It has to be planted in soil that is moist, fertile, and at the right temperature, and it has to get the proper amount of water and sunlight. If these conditions are present, the seed will begin to grow. Once the plant breaks through

the ground to the surface, it will not only still need these conditions met, but must also be protected from the harsh elements of
wind and rain, and threats from animals and man. If it can survive
all of this and continues to be properly nurtured each day, it will
grow into a large tree that can bear fruit for years.

Now let's look at this analogy for every true intention that
you hold in your mind right now. Each intention you have is like a
seed. The intention could relate to romance, money, career, health,
spiritual growth, or any number of other things. For each of these
intentions, there are conditions that need to come together for the
intention to manifest into a tangible and experiential reality. Learning these conditions is what life is really all about. It is the whole
purpose for suffering, mistakes, and failure. This is the process that
allows each one of us to develop the consciousness required to make
the choices that lead us to what we intend. **Therefore, TIME is
related to awareness.**

> "If you plant crab apples, don't count on harvesting Golden
> Delicious."
>
> —BILL MEYER

SOME INDIVIDUALS LEARN AT a much faster pace how to create
what they want out of life, while others make the same mistakes
and suffer the same painful consequences many times over. Perhaps you have seen it happen to family members or friends, and all

you could do was shake your head in disbelief at the redundant behavior. This is one example of how each of us pace our own evolution. Everyone is on his or her own "timetable" toward answers.

Science incorporates this process of trial and error all of the time; however, scientists recognize failure as a necessary part of the process of figuring out what works. Often, we get frustrated by failure and consider ourselves to be failures as a result. Mental scars to our self-worth inflicted in our youth can often become the overriding narrative during much of our lives. These misinterpreted experiences can have damaging effects in many ways. They can prevent us from having healthy relationships, keep us from getting over addictions, prevent us from taking better care of our bodies, deter us from running a successful business, and so on. **The time it takes to attain the things we desire, and the choices we make in the attempt to get there, are directly related to how we frame who we are.**

In my first book, *I AM: The Power of Discovering Who You Really Are*, I talk at length about the process of identity formation and its impact on our choices and how our lives unfold. The exciting thing is that when your will for a change is greater than your fear of a change, you will open your eyes to the answers that have been waiting for you. Time then collapses as the barrier of ignorance that had kept you from making new choices also dissipates. You are no longer preventing yourself from creating and aligning with what your true heart desires.

LET'S LOOK AT A FEW real-life examples that show how important it is to not only make the choices that build the conditions for your intention, but also make sure you do not dilute these conditions. The idea is to make sure you are aware of what needs to be done each day.

Taking the seed example further, we can see how important it is to be aware of what is necessary to make the vision real. The seed itself represents an intention. Let's say it's an apple seed. As mentioned earlier, three or four critical things are needed for this seed to "flower" and grow into a fruitful tree. With the consistent application of these conditions, the seed should start to open, take root, and eventually grow. The size, color, taste, and quantity of the fruit it will bear will all be influenced in some way by how this seed was nurtured since it was first planted. We could even go a bit deeper in this analogy and say that the power of the seed itself is based on how this particular type of seed has been cultivated over generations of time.

Similarly, individuals are shaped by the generations of people who came before them. Their DNA has evolved over time to ensure survival. What was passed to them was shaped by what genetic coding worked for each previous generation. This combined with their upbringing (nurturing) has made them who they are today.

Just like a human being, the seed is powerfully influenced by the way it is nurtured from the moment it is planted, regardless of its evolutionary history. What will have the biggest impact on the plant and its fruit is the attention, time, and effort that go into the nurturing process. This is a vital analogy that applies to many aspects of life. For an evergreen tree, proper nourishment (or lack thereof) could mean the difference between it becoming the one that is the magnificent Christmas tree displayed at Rockefeller Center or one that ends up like the Christmas tree in the *Charlie*

Brown Christmas special. The main point is that nurturing has a critical impact on results. The awareness exhibited during the nurturing of any intention plays a major role in how what you are looking to have happen unfolds. Cultivating the perfect conditions requires intense attention to detail. You must really be conscious of the energy that you are exhibiting at all times.

For example, you may think you planted your seed in fertile soil and go on for years not realizing that the reason the seed didn't grow because what you thought was fertile soil was actually soil completely devoid of nutrients. The seed never had a chance.

You may have thought you were watering the tree with fresh water each day, but later realized the water was tainted and unhealthy.

To bring the analogy back to some life situations, you may have thought you were doing the right thing building confidence in your child by pushing them to be "perfect" in school, sports, and hobbies, not realizing that the pressure he was under caused him to lose confidence in himself, not gain it.

You may have thought you were demonstrating love in your relationship by buying your partner expensive gifts, not realizing that being present and open to your partner's deeper emotional needs was actually a more powerful way to create the deeper love and connection you wanted.

These are much more subtle and sneaky ways that the ego keeps us from a grander sense of fulfillment while at the same time allowing us to go on believing that we are doing all we can do. Confusion is often the result. **If what you really desire is not taking shape, remember that there is always a specific reason why. Never be afraid to find that reason!**

**This May Be a Good Time to Reflect and Ask
Yourself a Few Very Important Questions:**

- What are some of the roles you have been playing through-out your life, at work, in your relationships, with your parents, siblings, or kids that you don't want to play anymore?
- Do these roles serve you now based on what you desire for your life?
- Are you ready for real change?
- Are you willing to redefine who you are, hold yourself in a higher regard, and begin to act and respond to life in a different way?
- Are you ready to build a new set of conditions through your daily choices?

HERE ARE A FEW EXAMPLES OF how the mind works in conjunction with your most protected truths about who you are. If you believe you lack a sense of value in your relationships, you will nurture this feeling into your experience. You will cultivate relationships that will devalue you in some way, and instead of acknowledging this, you will make excuses for them. Or, you will ignore some of your own behaviors that cause them to disconnect with you in some way. This could be anything from your attitude to your energy. Your story of limited value will be validated. This will continue until you no longer tolerate what is happening and decide it's time for change.

IF YOU CONTINUE TO SEE yourself as limited in your dealings with money, your world will fulfill this for you. It will show up in the poor conditions of your employment, in the poor choices you make with large purchases, and in the unchecked spending habits of yourself or your family. You will nurture the conditions that keep you feeling repressed financially. Time will stretch in that it will take you longer to move forward on the road to a completely different financial picture.

If you believe in a poor self-image, you will subconsciously look to get this type of feedback. You will make excuses for your diet, you will lack the motivation to stay in shape, and you will present yourself in a way that triggers negative responses and feedback from yourself and others. The time it takes to become healthy and physically fit will expand.

The energy of your truth draws the truth-affirming conditions toward you and your reality in every moment. The all-powerful elegance of the universe is working with you 24/7 to help you validate your existence in a million different ways, shapes, and forms. The implications of this realization are endless. To one who comes to embrace the true power in this understanding, fear recedes and the idea of time dissolves. A new trust in life allows for new possibilities to be entertained and old limiting thoughts to lose their impact. Your dreams no longer become a matter of if or when; rather, you will be focused only on the beauty, perfection, and opportunity to create that is right now. Faith takes over and puts you squarely in the flow of life.

The power behind realizing that life works with you is found in a mind that focuses on personal possibility over limits. It is found in the actions that work to form new conditions. There is no more fear in the consequences of seeing the truth of your current circumstances. There is no more fear in creating a new set of conditions and dealing with change. There is no fear in trying or failing in order to learn what conditions aren't being met. Dr. Jonas Salk, the creator of the polio vaccine, failed many times before he succeeded at his discovery. His persistence and belief through the failures allowed him to eventually come to a moment where he put all the right conditions together. Millions and millions have been relieved of suffering and have benefited as a result.

> "Nothing happens quite by chance. It's a question of accretion of information and experience."
>
> —Jonas Salk

This is the case with many of the things in your life that you would like to change in a shorter amount of time. You must be willing to fail. You must overcome your fear of change for the conditions to change. Fear works against you when it comes to building a new reality. Fear repels the information that would lead you to what you desire. Faith, however, attracts these necessary conditions!

This is not the blind faith often used by people who do not want to take responsibility for their actions and hope their problems or challenges will simply take care of themselves. This is a much more practical faith that says you trust the way the universe conspires to help you turn thought into reality. This does not mean you won't have to face some hard facts about what is currently possible; rather, it means you are willing to accept any truth with a personal love and trust that help you always to move forward in new thought and action.

IN THE EXAMPLE of Dewey Bozella, he had to face the truth that attaining his freedom and the recognition of his innocence would involve a certain process. He did not let any negative thoughts about the difficulty of the task or the amount of time it would take to achieve his desires impede him from his goal. He worked from right where he was. He used his time wisely in jail. He got a good education, got married, and became a boxing champion, all while falsely imprisoned and working hard for the freedom he truly believed in for himself.

In this very moment, and most likely under much less dire circumstances than Dewey Bozella found himself in, you have the same opportunity to change everything. With a strong will, a healthy dose of self-love, and a clear vision of what you desire, you are on your way. The infinite possibility that exists in this very moment awaits you.

THESE ARE FOUR KEYS to immediately begin building the vital conditions that will allow you to fulfill your desire and shorten the experience of "time" in the process:

1. You must be willing to look at all past actions that created your present circumstance with total understanding
   and without any regret, guilt, or shame.

   You must know the consequence and the karma of
   your past actions, but you must also know that your
   greatest gift resides in a new idea of who you are now.
   This is the moment of your perfection. This awareness
   is critical to the liberating self-love that will send out a
   new creative energy today. It is also imperative to learn
   from what did not work for you and incorporate those
   key lessons into today's choices.

2. You must be totally honest about where you are now in
   relation to what you truly desire.

   Delusion is one of the ego's biggest tools. Life often
   presents you with situations that humble you to the exact
   degree that you were deluded about the truth. You know
   the Rolling Stones lyric, "You can't always get what you
   want . . . But if you try sometime, you might just find
   you get what you need."

   While you may not yet know everything you'll need
   on your journey, being honest about the road ahead and
   where you are in the process will give you the space to
   learn, rather than stopping progress by thinking you
   know it all.

   **Humility is a powerful attribute as it relates to wis-
   dom.** Those who can say "I don't know" when they truly
   don't understand end up getting the wisdom they need
   a lot faster than those who say "I know" when they really
   don't have a clue. The fear of not knowing and the lie

that's often used as a cover ironically work against them and close off the door to true wisdom.

3. You must be completely open to action, temporary failure, and change.

Those who powerfully achieve what they desire are willing to risk the status quo for something even greater for themselves. Time is secondary to the desire to create and change their current circumstance. They thrive on failure and look forward to what they can learn, and how they can grow and adapt. Change is welcomed, not feared, and this is what allows them to take unrestricted action toward the dream. Any result is seen as part of the journey toward the ultimate goal, *which is never in doubt.*

"Forget safety. Live where you fear to live. Destroy your reputation. Be notorious."

—Rumi

4. You must have the will to move forward no matter what challenges or setbacks you face.

You will be challenged on your journey. You may be challenged by many truths about yourself that you will have to face. You may be challenged by the limiting beliefs and opinions of other people who can't dream as big as you can. You may be challenged by the nature of divine timing, the need for patience, and the trap of fear. You also may be challenged along the way by things that don't go according to plan and by the need to adapt to current circumstances. Each of these challenges will require an unwavering will to move forward.

> "The most essential factor is persistence—the determination to never allow your energy or enthusiasm to be dampened by the discouragement that must inevitably come."
>
> —James Whitcomb Riley

A CONSISTENT APPLICATION of these four conditions is ultimately what gives birth to any intended reality. The quicker the conditions come together, the shorter the time of gestation. Once all the conditions are in place, there is nothing left to do but have pure faith in the process of life.

In a place that is beyond the limits of the mind, all is possible. The journey you are on now is about opening up to more of what life is offering you every day. Each desire that comes to the forefront of your mind has its own set of truths that need to be accepted before that desire can become a reality. You are worthy.

Since your degree of self-love will always dictate your experience, the path to realizing more of your true worth, perfection, and creative capability is the key to it all. There is no difference between you and anyone else on this entire planet when it comes to possibility and worthiness. Yes, we all come from different starting points and circumstances, but every human being has the free will to decide what they will create from their experience and how they will go about it. In this never-ending moment, creation and time are in your hands.

Ye Are Gods

You are the creator
Your reality birthed by your beliefs
Conceived by the infinite intercourse of observation and perception
That leads to an endless experience
The type and style is of your free will.
Are you producing
Hatemaking or lovemaking?
Ignorance or awareness?
Fear or faith?
It has always served you.
Does it now?
You are the creator
Holding the future in your hands
Changing it with every thought
Changing it with every desire
Changing it with every act
Time does not exist
There's always time.

PART IV

TRANSCENDING TIME

(Discovering Eternal Joy)

"Time is
Too slow for those who wait,
Too swift for those who fear,
Too long for those who grieve,
Too short for those who rejoice;
But for those who Love,
Time is not."

—HENRY VAN DYKE

TRUSTING
CIRCUMSTANCE

A big part of stepping into a place of true joy in life comes when you realize how life is always working *for* you. It can be very liberating to know that things do not just happen to you. Even the most painful experiences have meaning and purpose. When you truly understand this, the benefit it has in your life is enormous. The resistance that was the source of much of your mental and physical pain begins to subside. Trust and faith are what guide you through dark periods, making them less painful and allowing you to get back into the flow of life much more quickly. A lighter, more hopeful feeling begins to take over.

I'm sure you can think of many people in your life who went through a tough situation that robbed them of years of joy. Maybe it was a bad breakup that took them years to accept, a sudden change in career, tough economic times, or a health crisis. Instead of accepting the circumstance, trusting and putting the best energy they could toward moving forward, they chose to resist truth and dwell on what could have been, what should have been, or what would have been.

There is always a choice. In order to gain control over time and the creation of your life, you must accept the truth that exists in each moment, and that includes trusting with unwavering faith that all circumstances have a purpose and reason behind them. **There isn't anything you experience in reality that is not for you in some way.**

WE HAVE ALL HEARD the saying, "Be careful what you wish for, because you just might get it." What this means is that immediately upon the birth of an intention, conditions begin to form, even if you can't see them. Challenges, tragedy, positive experiences, and negative ones come together to help feed you the awareness you need. Being ready by simply trusting that the universe supports you in every possible way can make a huge difference during any challenge you are confronted with.

- It can affect the degree of pain from the experience.
- It can affect the timetable of the experience.
- It can positively or negatively affect many other lives by the way you choose to handle the circumstance.
- It can affect the outcome of the experience.

WHEN THINKING ABOUT THE NOTION of trusting life you may want to dedicate some time to seriously contemplating the following statement:

How can you not trust a universe that has birthed you into existence?

THE ATOMS AND MOLECULES from which you are made have been through an endless amount of transformation and change just to be right here, right now in the form of you. This improbable journey has led to this moment and this amazing space of support and love. A trillion different coincidences all came together over the expanse of time to form you and everything around you right now. There is an enormous purpose for your existence. You have an effect on everything you put your attention on. This is how crucial you are as the eyes to the world. This is how vital you are as the eternal observer of life. This is how loved you are, how much you matter, and how important you are to the creation of your reality and to the impact you have had, are having, and will have on millions of other people.

The question is never one of *if you matter* as an individual experience of consciousness, but rather of *how you will CHOOSE to matter* in your world from this very moment onward. This is a big part of mastering your reality. This is a very important part of mastering "time."

SIGNIFICANT OTHERS, family members, children, friends, and strangers all count on you to play a certain role and to have a certain impact on their lives. What if you chose right here and right now to play only the most trusting and loving role possible to them? No longer resisting many things you face every day, but accepting the truth of the circumstance and operating from this powerful place of universal harmony. This certainly doesn't mean you must condone any situation that does not agree with who you are, but rather you acknowledge its existence and then play the most powerful role you can to positively affect the situation in a loving and compassionate way.

> **Challenges reveal the gap between what you say you want and what you've yet to understand and overcome as it relates to creating what you want.**

LIFE WILL PUT YOU to the test. This is an inescapable part of the process. Some of these tests will be minor and without incident, while others will be bigger challenges you will have to deal with. Your ability to overcome is greater than you can ever imagine. There have been millions before you who have suffered tragedy and survived, and in many cases, even thrived as a result. You have this same capability, no matter what you face and how you decide to use "time" through the process.

It is critical to understand that all challenges have extremely valuable information buried in them. Without a circumstance to reflect upon and question, there is no way the information or awareness could make its way into your consciousness. **When it comes to awareness, the truth of how it had to happen is self-evident in what happened.**

Some of these challenges may be very painful at first. This is when it is vital to remember all you have to be grateful for in your life. This is when perspective becomes a doorway to peace. This is a time to reflect on your true infinite nature. You are beyond dissolution. While you may experience the finiteness of your body and the ending of many attachments in your world, who you are on a deeper spiritual or "soul" level is beyond any perceived limitation of time and space.

If you find yourself in one of life's more challenging situations, the following saying can be a *very* powerful reminder of your transcendence. It is for you to repeat as necessary—in the moments when you need to be reminded of the powerful nature of your existence. Think of it as a very sacred affirmation rolled up in one of those cases that reads, "In case of emergency, break glass." Use this affirmation when you need it most:

**I CAN AND I WILL BECAUSE
I AM.**

Life can throw us a challenge at any waking moment. In the process, it can change your life on a dime. Such a circumstance was thrust upon one of my very best friends in 2010.

MICHAEL HAD BEEN DEALING WITH a lot in life at the time. His father had passed away earlier in the year after a very long illness that took a lot emotionally out of Michael, his brother, and his mother. On top of this, Michael's business was struggling in the midst of the economic recession. It was a period of time in his life when the gravity of his situation drove him to ask bigger questions and face some significant changes. His ability to embrace all of this abrupt change was a process that was moving at a slower pace than he probably wished.

I remember exactly where I was when I got the call from his wife. Lying in bed, watching the news, I heard my cell phone buzz and picked it up. She said, "Howie, this is Laura. Michael's just been in a terrible car accident."

"How is he?!" I immediately responded. My heart seemed to slow to a stop as I waited for her next words, knowing they would tell me the gravity of the situation.

"He's going to make it, but he needs many surgeries. Howie, in the accident, he completely lost his left arm from the shoulder down."

There are rare occasions in life when you witness or experience things that you can't seem to wrap your mind around at first. Things we don't ever want to see or hear about. This was one of those moments.

After a very long pause as I tried to take it all in, I asked, "What can I do to help?"

"He has a few more surgeries scheduled over the next few days [he had been through two already and ended up having more than nine before he was released], but he is going to need some major mental support, and I'm not sure I'll be able to handle it," she said in an anxious and understandably desperate tone. "I could use some help."

"I'm on my way," was my response. And with that, I booked a flight to Chicago in the next twenty-four hours.

After I hung up, my thoughts immediately went to his two

young boys, ages thirteen and ten at the time. How were they handling all this? I was thankful, on one hand, that their father was alive, but also completely unsure how he and his family would cope with the new normal. **I knew that the single most important factor influencing how they would handle what had happened to their father was how their father would handle what had happened to him.**

The next morning, I woke up and had an idea. Before I got out of bed, I took my left hand, placed it behind my back, and decided to not move it or use it for the rest of the day. I got up, went to the bathroom, and washed my hand and face. I brushed my teeth (holding the toothbrush handle in my teeth while I applied toothpaste). I made breakfast. I could not tie my shoes so I put on slip-ons. Next, I got into the car and drove to the local golf course. One of the things his wife had said to me on the phone the night before was that she hoped he'd be able to do the things he loved to do again. Golf was one of Michael's passions. I took my golf bag out of my trunk, slung it over my right shoulder, went into the pro shop, and bought a bag of practice balls. Getting money out of my wallet was a bit of a challenge on the first try, but I knew with practice it would become easier. I went down to the range, teed up my first ball—all with my left arm still behind my back—and took my first swing. Crack! Right down the middle. Not 250 yards down the middle, but straight and in the 150-to-175-yard range—surprisingly long, considering that I had no idea whether I'd be able to hit the ball even halfway decently with the use of just one arm.

After hitting some more balls and trying a few different clubs,

I got back in the car and drove home. I then took a shower, washed my hair, dried off, and got fully dressed—all with my left arm held behind my back. I now knew I could at least walk into the hospital in Chicago, look Michael straight in the eyes, and tell him that while he was obviously going to experience a significant adjustment to life, he would be fine. Could I speak to the physical pain he was feeling from the nerve damage? No. Could I speak to the deep emotional pain of going through this type of loss and the grieving process that would be a part of it? No. Could I speak to the changes in balance and body temperature that he would be dealing with in the days and weeks to come? No. Could I speak to the mental process of adjusting to this new physical identity? No. Nor would I ever attempt to. This personal process was his to deal with and respond to as he chose. But could I look at him, his wife, kids, and mother and tell them that he would be able to do most of the things he could do before? Yes. Could I tell them he would still be able to take care of himself the same way most people do? Yes.

In the midst of tragic situations, people's minds often focus on the worst-case scenario. In Michael's situation, at least I could alleviate some of the deep fears he and his family were having about how he would return to his day-to-day activities with just one arm.

Two days after the accident, I arrived at the hospital, took a deep breath, and walked into Michael's room. Tears streamed down both our faces when we saw each other. Michael and I had been friends since kindergarten and had known each other since we were three years old. Although our families moved apart when we were still in grade school, we had always remained the closest of friends. I walked to his bedside, gave him a kiss on the forehead, and sat down next to him. After a long moment of silence, he looked at me and asked, "How am I going to get through this, Howie?" I looked right at him and firmly replied, "However you choose to."

Something deep within him seemed to understand. And over the course of the next three days, in between visits from many people, we had deep discussions that covered it all: the guilt he felt about putting his wife and kids through this, and his fears of what life might be like from this moment forward.

AT THE CORE, how his life would unfold in the aftermath of the accident depended on the answers to some powerful key questions. Keep in mind as you read them that this not only applied to Michael, but also applies to you, the reader, in whatever situation you face in your life right now.

- What is your intention?
- How quickly can you accept the truth and the reality of what is?
- How much can you find to be grateful for despite the difficult circumstances you face?
- How open are you to see what is being offered in what is happening?

- How will you choose to define who you are in response to what is?
- How much willpower and faith can you demonstrate each day based on what is?

THE ANSWERS TO THESE QUESTIONS determine it all. The way you interpret and feel about the current situation, combined with your response and efforts each day, lay the groundwork for the life you build. So many are affected each day by how you choose to define who you are. In Michael's case, he started from a place of gratitude for all he did have. The fact that his life had been spared in the accident was a miracle in itself.

While driving down a two-lane highway on a gorgeous Chicago morning, a flatbed construction truck crossed the median and hit Michael head-on, crushing the whole left side of his car. Michael was in a convertible and had his left arm hanging leisurely out the window. He had no time to react.

After the collision, a man named Eric, who had been two cars behind him, ran up and saw that Michael was unconscious, that his left arm had been severed, and that he was rapidly losing blood. Miraculously, and I do mean miraculously, Eric had the wherewithal to get a few people around him to grab some twigs from nearby trees, and fashion them and a few rags into a tourniquet. He fastened the tourniquet around what remained of Michael's left shoulder and stemmed the bleeding. This calm, responsive, and clearheaded act ended up saving Michael's life. Two to three more minutes of blood loss and he would have been dead.

Eric and his family have since become very close friends with Michael and his family. As providence would have it, Eric wasn't even supposed to be in town or driving down that particular road that day. A few chance days off from work and his decision to take a scenic detour that day made all the difference in the world to Michael and his loved ones. Also, it turned out this wasn't the first time that Eric had been at the right place at the right time to save somebody's life. In fact, this was his third time!

Yes, there are angels among us.

On the last day of my visit, Michael and I came up with a statement of intention for him to remember every day. This was to be used as a powerful guiding reaffirmation of truth and purpose as Michael went through the process of embracing a new identity. There was certainly a long road ahead for him as he learned to deal with the full reality of losing his arm. Physical pain became part of his day-to-day experience and would still be a challenge in the weeks and months ahead. Michael's incredibly strong will to tackle each situation head-on and with the best attitude he could muster, however, served not only to speed up his healing process, but also affected, in an immeasurable way, the well-being of his wife, mother, and two wonderful children. In addition, there have been hundreds, if not thousands, of people in his hometown who have been inspired by his amazing attitude and grace in dealing with what he has faced. He continues to be a source of inspiration for many who feel they have problems that are too big to overcome.

This reminds me of the old saying, "I used to be down because I had no shoes, until I saw a man who had no feet."

MICHAEL'S AFFIRMATION READS:

"I AM grateful that I AM alive. I choose to not only heal, but to thrive as a result; therefore, I choose to fully accept what has happened to me and my left arm. I AM grateful for my life, my wife, my children, my family, my friends, and all the love that surrounds me each day. I AM blessed and realize that there is a tremendous opportunity in front of me to inspire and positively affect many people if that is the road I choose to take. I understand that I have the power to shape the experience of the rest of my life in any way that I desire. Most important, I know that who I AM is not defined by anything physical but always by who I choose to be as a human being in this very moment.

I choose to see only love, gratitude, opportunity, and endless possibility every day for the rest of my life. Amen."

HONORING NOW

Try as we might, we cannot catch a moment. We can capture it in memory, in feeling, on video, and in photographs, but we cannot freeze one or prevent the next one from happening. This is the eternal birth of the universe moment to moment. This is the ongoing experience of creation. Life constantly moves forward.

Many times, when a person has had an experience that has created a certain feeling of bliss or great joy, they do everything in their power to try to re-create or "get back to" this same state of mind. This bliss could have been the result of an experience with certain drugs that eventually caused an addiction. This feeling could have come from falling deeply in love, but then may have led to a codependent relationship. Or this feeling of nirvana could have been achieved in a state of deep meditation.

The danger of trying to re-create these experiences is that you are usually looking to achieve the same state of mind rather than focusing on a new creative experience that actually produces a very similar feeling. These incredible experiences come from participating in the HERE and NOW, not trying to re-create yesterday. The feeling of timelessness or endless joy comes not from searching for this mental state but from actively participating in life and immersing yourself in this moment as you work toward your greatest hopes and dreams.

THE MORE YOU CAN FOCUS on what is happening right now, the faster the conditions will come together to produce the joy you craved in the first place. Joy does not come by forcing it to happen. It comes by consistently accepting the nature of what is in front of you at this moment, honoring this gift and responding to it as powerfully as you can—in the way that defines who you choose to be.

For example, if you are let go from your job or denied a promotion, you can choose to build drama around the situation, or you can respond by redefining who you know that you are and taking direct action for immediate change. Maybe this challenge is the final straw that moves you to make ten phone calls to other companies that would be thrilled to have you work for them. Maybe this is what moves you to have a talk with management about your goals to see if they are even aware or on board with what role you would like to play in the company.

Take a Moment to Contemplate the Following:

What does this very moment mean to you?

Can you see the sacredness of this precious instance in time?

Can you feel the universe talking to you and responding to some of your deepest questions?

Do you realize how much you matter and how loved you are by "life"?

THE GOAL OF EACH MOMENT is a simple one. It is to allow you the space to discover more and more of *who you really are* and what is truly possible for you. It is to offer you insight and to allow you to discover the answers to some of the questions you have asked about your life. This moment is showing you how to create life in a more peaceful, loving, and creatively fulfilling way!

Time is the constant experience of the space between who you think that you are and who you are destined to become.

HONORING NOW IS ABOUT HONORING life. Every answer to every question you have asked exists in this moment. Access to these answers is about being ready for the shift in awareness and the true change that will occur if you allow these answers into your consciousness. Embracing this new information is a matter of really wanting it and truly trusting it. It is about feeling absolutely worthy and ready for it. Honor, respect, and unconditional self-love are key. **It is about the end of judgment of yourself, and hence, the end of judgment of your world.**

SEEING THE WORLD THROUGH THE eyes of pure love is very powerful. It allows you to see meaning everywhere, as though you were a child who had no preconceived notions, ideas, or judgment of the world. All that you perceive is seen for the gift that it offers on your journey to becoming a master creator of your own destiny.

T HERE IS A VERY APPROPRIATE Zen teaching story I'd like to share with you about being in this state of non-judgment and openness to what is in front of you. This story is called "The Holy Man."

Word spread across the countryside about a wise Holy Man who lived in a small house at the very top of a nearby mountain. A man from the village who was very interested in learning this Holy Man's secrets decided to make the long and difficult journey up the mountain to visit him.

When he arrived at the house, an old man who appeared to be a servant greeted him at the door and led him inside. "I would like you to take me to see the wise Holy Man," he said to the servant.

The servant smiled and led him inside. As they walked through the house, the man from the village looked eagerly around, desperately anticipating his encounter with the Holy Man.

Before he knew it, he had been led to the back door and escorted outside. He stopped, turned to the servant, and demanded, "But I want to see the Holy Man!"

"You already have," said the old man. "Take notice of everyone you meet in life, even if they appear plain and insignificant, for they may have valuable information or an important lesson for you to learn. See each person you encounter in life as a holy person and the solutions to whatever problems you have brought here today will be solved."

HOW MANY TIMES HAS LIFE delivered you answers only for you to have them go unnoticed, ignored, or denied? How exciting is it to realize that you are now preparing yourself to see more of them as you realize the perfection of the matrix of all of life? A big part of what makes life majestic is that it is always working to honor your highest requests. You have asked many questions. You have been searching for the answers. Your cries have not gone unheard. It is just that the letters you have been receiving have been left unopened. When the student is ready . . .

HONORING NOW IS ABOUT the end of judgment and the ability to fully trust the perfection of everything that is happening now. It is about realizing the infinite possibilities that exist for you right in this very moment as you read these words! Honoring NOW is to be excited about being alive and having the eternal opportunity to learn what you need to know to feel at peace and in balance with life. When you immerse yourself in this sacred moment, the divinity of all things shines through. This is when your own divinity shines through. Pressure and time then just melt away.

LIVING TIMELESSLY
AND FEARLESSLY

Do you remember the feeling when you were at an amusement park and you finally got to the front of the line for the big roller coaster? A huge amount of anticipation built as you were about to get on the ride. You got in your seat, and you strapped yourself in or pulled the security bar down right before the roller coaster started to move at a very high speed. At that moment your whole body and mind prepared for what was about to happen. You were more excited than scared, or you wouldn't have been on the ride. You were alive with anticipation and enthusiastic about the experience in front of you. This is exactly what living timelessly and fearlessly is all about.

This way of living is about crossing the boundary from fear to faith, from worry to trust, from limit to limitless. **It is about fully letting go and trusting a universe that has delivered you through every other trying time and circumstance to this moment in your life.**

. . .

YOU CAN'T LIVE TIMELESSLY and *then* fearlessly. It only works the other way around. Because time is a result of perception, perception is not a result of time. Trust is a huge factor in the dissolution of fear. You must trust that life is a self-supporting, self-sustaining journey. And while there will be more learning experiences and moments of pain in life, *there will always be a light at the end of the tunnel*. The sun will always rise and a new day will dawn. With it will be a smarter and more aware, mature, and experienced you.

REMOVING THE OBSTACLES that have been in the way of what you have been trying to create requires you to face your fears, challenge your old beliefs, and step into new, and generally uncomfortable, territory. It requires you to be willing to take the full plunge regardless of what new fears emerge and what new truths you must face along the way. Many have done this before you. There are endless examples from history of people who have achieved incredible things. Each of these journeys has been wrought with burdens, fears, and great challenges along the way.

The analogy of a mountain climber is a very appropriate one here. There have been countless individuals who have attempted to climb Mount Everest, only to have to turn back when they were halfway or three-quarters of the way there—or even when the summit was within sight. But for those who were determined, this was not the end of their journey. Like swimmer Diana Nyad, they recovered and attempted their goal again. They weathered the storms, the cold, the exhaustion, and every fear imaginable along the way. They demonstrated the power of the human spirit to overcome. The reward of this persistence and faith was the ability to plant their flag on the top of the mountain. They got to feel the priceless feeling of satisfaction by the achievement of a lifelong intention or dream.

> "It is not the mountain that we conquer but ourselves."
> —SIR EDMUND HILLARY

Your path toward your goals is no different. The process of creation also may hold some significant challenges for you. You may have already been through a number of your own storms in life. Each event provided you with a certain nugget of understanding. Each may have given you a new strength or a new perspective on life and what is important to you. They may have graced you with an increase in resolve. This is a very important thing to remember as you work now to tackle the new challenges in front of you.

Living fearlessly does not mean being in a state of ignorance or denial, but just the opposite. It means being willing to put one foot in front of the other each day, fully aware that you are doing your best to learn as you go. Excited about what amazing new insight could be revealed to you today! You are in the full trust of life. In an open state of mind, you know what you MUST do to make your dream a reality, and you do not let fear stop you.

As a matter of fact, noticing where you let fear stop you is one of the best indicators of where you have built a wall to your own dream. Fear ends up becoming a great sign of what your next move should be. You must look the imaginary dragon in the eye. The obstacle shows up to reveal where you may be limiting your own evolution of consciousness and identity.

Here Are a Few Questions to Consider:
- Do you know what your next step should be?
- What lie, rationalization, or excuse is holding you back from taking decisive action?
- Are you willing to tolerate another day of living under the same false fear?
- Do you want to be dealing with the same circumstances days or weeks from now?

THE CONNECTION BETWEEN the elimination of fear and the collapse of time is a simple one. Fearlessness means that you no longer worry about your survival. You understand a greater truth about your infinite nature. You also understand a greater truth about life's infinite nature. You no longer see limits on the creative capacity of life, in which you play a major part. Limitlessness means that you have full faith and trust in who you are and what you are capable of manifesting for yourself.

STEVE JOBS's 2005 commencement address at Stanford University encapsulates what it means to live fearlessly and in a state of perpetual creation:

When I was seventeen, I read a quote that went something like: "If you live each day as if it was your last, someday you'll most certainly be right." It made an impression on me, and since then, for the past thirty-three years, I have looked in the mirror every morning and asked myself: "If today were the last day of my life, would I want to do what I am about to do today?" And whenever the answer has been "no" for too many days in a row, I know I need to change something. Remembering that I'll be dead soon is the most important tool I've ever encountered to help me make the big choices in life. Because almost everything—almost everything—all external expectations, all pride, all fear of embarrassment or failure—these things just fall away in the face of death, leaving only what is truly important. Remembering that you are going to die is the best way I know to avoid the trap of thinking you have something to lose. You are already naked. There is no reason not to follow your heart.

LIVING FROM THIS LIBERATING STATE of mind produces unwavering and focused action. Steve Jobs's creative work was a testament to his statement. When you live your life this way, you don't see time as working against you anymore, but rather working for you—each challenge seen for its value, each failure embraced as an important part of the process.

In this state, you become like water that looks to keep flowing. The more water flows, the more powerful it becomes, as it carves through any obstacle along its way. When you are in a pure state of flow you don't see anything as an obstacle that can stop you anymore. When water stops flowing, it stagnates and produces algae, harmful bacteria, and disease. By continuously moving and flowing, water stays in its purest and most powerful form. Yes, there may be significant challenges in your life that may alter your path, but these incidents can never keep you and your will from moving in the most effective and timeless way possible.

Something very magical happens through the demonstration of a consistent will in the face of much adversity and struggle in life. The by-product is a strong demonstration of faith. In many ways, faith and the truth are the same, for what you have faith in is what you believe to be true. No matter what you go through, faith will always be your greatest and most valuable tool for survival and resilience.

THE FOLLOWING STORY EPITOMIZES the intangible and elegant nature of this formidable state of mind:

The Wise Woman—Author Unknown

A wise woman who was traveling in the mountains found a very precious stone in a stream. The next day, she met another traveler who was hungry, so the wise woman opened her bag to share her food. The hungry traveler saw the precious stone and asked the woman to give it to him. She did so without hesitation. The traveler left, rejoicing in his good fortune. He knew the stone was worth enough to give him security for a lifetime. But a few days later he came back to return the stone to the woman. "I've been thinking," he said. "I know how valuable the stone is, but I give it back in the hope that you can give me something even more precious. Can you give me what you have within you that enabled you to give me the stone?"

EITHER YOU HAVE FAITH IN life or you don't. This will be demonstrated in the actions you take, and even more important, in the energy behind these actions. The woman in the story revealed an incredible understanding about life that allowed her to covet nothing. As a result of not needing anything, nothing could be taken away from her, and in the universe's perfection the stone was returned. The universe is always mirroring your truth, as evidenced by how things come together in your life. The willingness to eventually adopt a fearless and trusting attitude is what opens the door to a new way of living, a new way of treating others, and, in turn, a new way that others treat you.

Your fate is always based on your faith in who you are.

IF YOU WERE TO REALLY think hard about it, how many things could you accomplish in the next twenty-four hours to get the ball rolling in the direction of your desires? How much change could literally begin to happen overnight? Once again, this is not just about the creation of physical things; it is also about your state of mind and general attitude about life.

For example, if you are looking for greater peace of mind, but it seems elusive, what five things could you implement in your daily routine to help you experience more peace? Could you spend

15 to 30 minutes in meditation each day? Could you cut caffeine or sugar from your diet to help your body feel more relaxed? Could you continue to learn to love and appreciate who you are and what you have been through in your life? Could you start getting up early and going for a walk in the quiet, peaceful morning? Could you find thirty minutes a day to exercise? These five simple ideas could change your experience of life if you chose to implement them immediately. This is how much you control time.

There is so much possibility available to you in this very moment. All you have to do to realize this potential is to look at all of the life around you. You will see the endless manifestations that have emerged from this limitless field of potential. All of it—every single thing in your existence—originated with intention. There is a beautiful tapestry that works through all things. This same divine tapestry works through you. As you learn to live from more of a limitless and loving mind-set, you no longer wait for the time to be right. You smile at the realization that the time is always right now.

> "The best time to plant a tree was twenty years ago. The second best time is now."
>
> —CHINESE PROVERB

SO WHAT IS THE OPTIMUM mind-set for being in the immaculate state of presence? What is the best attitude to embrace that puts time on your side in every waking moment of your existence? What way of understanding and being in the world fosters in you an energy that works in complete harmony with the universe to "collapse" time for you as it relates to your most desired experiences of life?

THE FOLLOWING ARE FIVE ATTITUDES to put you in the highest state of presence and creative energy. These attitudes cannot be faked. They must be authentic, stemming from a complete understanding and trust in the way your intentions are connected to what is happening in each moment.

Embracing these concepts produces an energy that attracts the conditions (people, places, and events) needed to lead you closer to what you want to experience. Earlier in the book, I discussed practices that stretch time and prevent your desires from coming to fruition. The following concepts collapse time and lead you toward what you desire.

Being in a state of disharmony is a sign that you are not in a place of remembrance of these concepts or the amazing and powerful state of grace they produce.

Acceptance

Energetic benefit: Dissolves any resistance to time and truth

Acceptance does not work at a deep level without understanding. Many "spiritual" teachings say that acceptance is needed to move forward and progress toward happiness. The major problem here is that the individual who has to accept the particular situation is still dogged by the deep need to see meaning behind it. The "Just accept it" line usually does not go over too well. This can be a huge impediment to progress and a contributing factor to the creation of more time and suffering. **The major purpose for any undesired or desired experience is to help expand one's awareness. Blind acceptance does nothing in this regard; rather, it's a forced attempt to find peace when the mind still wants to know "why?" Without the "why" answered, there may be no lasting acceptance or real peace.**

Without acceptance, there is resistance, and resistance causes the persistence of what you do not want to continue to exist. The reason behind every experience is to nudge you, or sometimes to shove you, to a greater awareness about life and what is possible for you. The journey reveals attachments, illusions, misunderstandings, and at the core, the ultimate truth that so much new possibility awaits you.

Many times, we experience the "why" weeks, months, and even years after the fact. But it does not have to be this way. You do not have to suffer for years in a state of misunderstanding and confusion. Learning how to live a more timeless and peaceful life is the whole point of this book. **Embracing the idea that everything that is happening or has happened has a divine reason behind it is a massive advancement in mastery over time and life.**

This does not mean you do not question what happens to you, but rather just the opposite! You question it from a place of working to understand the meaning for you and your advancement in consciousness. You do not question that it had to happen—you question *why* it had to happen. There is a huge difference between these two ways of thinking. If the lesson or awareness that any situation is here to give you could have happened another way for you, the simple and profound truth is that it would have.

Gratitude

Energetic benefit: Dissolves the belief in lack, making way for abundance

Feeling a sense of gratitude is an immediate way to gain perspective and shift to a more balanced state of mind. One of the main reasons for personal disharmony is the mind-set that you are not good enough or that you can't handle the circumstances you face. Turning your focus to the things you do have in your life right now, rather than the things you feel you do not have, brings more of a sense of hope and opportunity to the present moment.

No matter how bad your life feels now, there is always a situation in the world that can help shift your story. Turning on the evening news can immediately give you an improved perspective on your own life as you see the many unfortunate circumstances that are being reported on around the world. *Relativity* is a key word to understand here. Your mind-set is constantly being shaped by how you feel about yourself or how you perceive your current circumstance in relation to others'. The reflective mind is frequently comparing you and your circumstance to everyone and everything else in existence. This produces a context. Context gives you a measure, and it is this measure that you use to evaluate yourself against the rest of your world.

The practice to focus on here is one where you concentrate on always looking at what you have to be grateful for, not what you feel is missing in your life, for in truth nothing is ever missing. You can always find someone who you think has it better than you, and you can always find someone who you think has it worse. Which one you focus on and how it makes you feel determines the creative energy you put out in that moment. There are many everyday events we witness that give us this opportunity.

WHEN A TRAGEDY STRIKES ELSEWHERE, it tends to bring a sense of perspective as we reflect on our own lives. How many times do you need to see images of hurricanes, tsunamis, and earthquakes in different parts of the world to gain a broader perspective about your circumstance? Or, how about when you see news reports of areas of the world that seem constantly cursed with war and bloodshed? It can make your standard of living and your life seem not quite as dire as you originally may have thought.

Attending a funeral is always cause for some deep self-reflection. It is these significant events that motivate us to cherish the simple and amazing gift of life and to make a commitment to live it beautifully and peacefully, to not be held back by the previous limits of our minds, to learn to love freely and fully each day.

Experiencing the reality of the passing of another often moves us to appreciate what is really important regarding how we live our life now and how this relates to the legacy we leave. It is far beyond the money we accumulate or the accolades we receive. It is the impact we have on other people. This is the creative energy that transcends time and makes space for our spirit to live on.

Being grateful for the simple reality that you are alive can be a great starting point to shift to a more empowered state of mind.

A greater sense of gratitude and perspective produces the energy of understanding and acceptance. When your situation ignites some personal pain and confusion, your reality is nudging you toward a new way of thinking. It is pushing you to the greater truth of possibility, not limitation! Resistance or a lack of gratitude is often what is generating the suffering and time.

Suffering indicates that what you believe to be true about yourself or your circumstance is not the greater truth—thus, the purpose of your suffering.

THE ESSENCE OF PROGRESS FOR your life is always found in how you choose to interpret, react, and define yourself in the face of any challenge. If you choose to see the challenge before you as a sign that life is against you, this misunderstanding will add to the wall between you and what you desire. If you choose to walk in a path of humility and gratitude for each opportunity or challenge you face, you will learn faster, experience less pain, and conquer many more mountains. Each moment offers you this option!

Belief

Energetic benefit: Attracts new creative possibilities

Your mind is in a constant working relationship with your ego to confirm that what you believe to be true is real and experiential.

Therefore, a closed mind—or one that is not very open to new possibility—will look to confirm what can't be done. An open mind, however, will seek a world of new possibilities.

When you have a very strong belief in something, you do not "think" it is true; rather, you "know" it is true. You "know" it is going to happen. This knowing is expressed in the way you carry yourself. It shows itself in the way you respond to others. It exudes itself in all the energy you put out and in the way life responds back to you. It is demonstrated in the way you handle any adversity you face.

Having a powerful belief in yourself, your personal value, or in what you are trying to create is intoxicating to others. You can literally change someone else's mind by the energy of what you authentically believe to be true or demonstrate to be true. This is what the most famous leaders, athletes, and entrepreneurs in the world express. It is what some of the most famous men and women who changed history were able to do. They had a powerful vision or belief, and then they inspired others to make sure that vision came to fruition.

"Again, you cannot connect the dots looking forward; you can only connect them looking backwards. So you have to trust that the dots will connect in your future. You have to trust in something—your gut, destiny, life, karma, whatever. This approach has never let me down, and it has made all the difference in my life."

—STEVE JOBS

Any lack of belief will show up in a lack of action. There is no escaping this truth. Time then becomes more of a factor as weeks and months tick by with no progress. Once belief becomes strong enough and action is initiated, however, the wheels of creation and change start turning. Time is no longer a major factor. The magic of timeless creation takes over.

Faith

Energetic benefit: Absence of doubt allowing for a powerful certainty of mind that permits what you desire to become real

Fear works to repel the conditions that lead to what you desire, while faith attracts them. The reason is very simple. Fear emanates from a threat that is considered real and true, and life must respond to your truth. Therefore, your fear works to attract the conditions that fulfill the fear, and at the same time you consciously or subconsciously work to keep information away that would reveal the fear as false.

For example, if you fear getting fired from your job, that fear will negatively affect your energy and behavior at work and actually may lead to you getting fired. If you have faith in your abilities, however, this will allow you to work with certainty and confidence that no matter what happens, you will be OK. This will be the energy that leads you to a positive result.

If you have the fear of being rejected by your significant other, this need for constant validation and attention to alleviate your fear may put so much pressure on them that they eventually want to end the relationship. If you have faith in your value to the relationship and the love you give, however, this quiet confidence will exude an attraction that your significant other may never want to let go of.

Both fear and faith are self-fulfilling prophecies. Which one do you choose?

YOUR TRUE THOUGHTS not only have an effect on your decisions and choices, but because we are all connected, they have a profound effect on the decisions that others make in your reality. Others subconsciously know what you are looking to experience at the deepest level. They will treat you as such until you broadcast a different energy through your mind, body, and overall presence.

Your faith or lack thereof has a tangible effect on your reality and on your experience of "time." There is a paradox here: Real faith must come from a deeper understanding of life. Otherwise, you will try to force yourself to have faith just in the effort to be rewarded. You cannot, however, fool the universe. Your lack of faith or your fear will always be revealed. Your faith must be real and demonstrated consistently in who you are in each moment. You must learn at some point to let go and trust the outcome.

YOU WILL ENCOUNTER CHALLENGES in life. Your faith will be tested. The question is whether you will let circumstance limit what you see as possible or whether you will use the challenge to push yourself to a new level of belief in yourself. Will you use the experience to confirm that you live in a cold world of random chaos that seems to go against you, or will you have faith in your creative power and a giving, self-supportive, and loving universe that has a purpose for everything it puts in your path?

"Worry never robs tomorrow of its sorrow, it only saps today of its joy."

—LEO BUSCAGLIA

Love

Energetic benefit: Inner peace and the bonding agent of all positive experiences.

Love is the transformative power that encourages you to explore and become more of who you really are. This love is found in the passion you exhibit for any area of life. Acceptance, gratitude, belief, and faith are all vital components of mastering your reality. They are each important in creating positive energy. Unconditional love, however, is the glue of it all. It is what binds every coincidence and desired event in your life together. It is the core ingredient that drives the whole process. Often this love shows up as passion. "He has a passion for what he does that shows in all of his work." "She exudes so much passion in her art." "His passion for the sport allows him to do the impossible."

What you are passionate about is what your heart and soul are most creatively drawn to doing every day. Without a strong love or passion, you can feel like you are just going through the motions. Life can lose its meaning. Time can feel like it just drags on. Yes, you can still accomplish many goals, but the karmic back side is you experience no sense of true satisfaction or peace. Your soul and your spirit seem to be disconnected from your actions.

When you are passionate about what you desire to do, time is no longer a factor. There is an endless supply of energy you find to fulfill your passion. You feel alive and in the moment, and your spirit and soul seem to be in divine symmetry. Everything seems "right."

Experiencing passion is a result of coming to a greater sense of love, understanding, and acceptance of yourself. This is the only way that your true desires will have a chance to be believed in as an actual possibility for you. Even more important, this newfound self-understanding and respect give you the courage to direct your passion into your actions.

LOVING AND HONORING YOURSELF MORE and more each day is at the heart of the power you have to create for yourself. If you can find more love and appreciation for your life, you can find more gratitude for all of the life around you. Life can then simply respond to your creative desires rather than be forced to respond to your ignorance. It can produce a synchronistic energy with your environment that is always working to grace you with what you want.

WHILE WE ARE EACH INDIVIDUALS expressing ourselves in different ways, we could not experience the necessary contrast and self-reflection without each other. There is a thread that connects every human being and everything in matter. At the deepest level, there is no separation between any of us. Every one of us is playing a role and serving a purpose for others. The idea of separation is an expression of a certain amount of ignorance to this truth. Ignorance is what gives birth to "time" and suffering. The more you show appreciation and respect for this connection with others, the more they respond positively to this energy. These connections range from your family and friends to your waiter or the guy who fixes your car, from the angry customer to the busy employee at the drive-through. It can be fun to blast them with your energetic love and appreciation! Watch their eyes light up a bit as you offer this sincere inner acknowledgment.

Love, expressed both as a passion for what you want to create and as a respect and honor for all of life (both organic and inorganic), is so important because it sends out an energy of unity and harmony to everyone you interact with. The result of this expression is that you receive a reflection of this love back to you on a daily basis. The ways, shapes, and forms that this takes are impossible to count. Love creates a tremendous positive karma. The world honors your life and true passion by working with you in the great flow of life to help make it all a reality.

> "Where there is love there is life."
>
> —MAHATMA GANDHI

SMILING THROUGH
THE SILENCE

"Don't count the moments, make the moments count."

—Unknown

There will be times in your life that seem very quiet. You may be doing all you can do and following your path to the best of your ability, but it seems as if nothing is happening. This couldn't be further from the truth. Just because you can't see it or feel it does not mean that things are not working in your favor. Every day, every minute, and every hour, the necessary conditions and vital lines of connection are being formed.

There is a profound meaning in the silence. Maybe the purpose is to test how much faith you really have in life. A deep worry about time represents a misunderstanding. The feeling of not having enough time is rooted in the belief that there is no meaning in the present moment. If you do not believe there is meaning in this moment, life will show you the meaning by keeping you in the same recurring pattern, increasing your angst until you relent to a greater truth. By worrying about time, you will actually lose the precious moment in front of you. You will be stuck until you accept the sacred meaning of what is before you, thereby freeing yourself into a new moment.

> "Time is like a handful of sand—the tighter you grasp it, the more it runs through your fingers."
>
> —HENRY DAVID THOREAU

AFTER TILLING THE SOIL, planting the seeds, and watering, there is not much more the farmer can do. At this point it is up to the magic of creation. It is time to sit back and let the power of providence take over.

Silence offers you a great opportunity for self-reflection and the purging of all doubt. It is a time to demonstrate your unwavering faith in the process of the universe. It is always about the process, not time. If you are thinking of the time, you are not in the process. Thinking about time actually adds to the experience of it, for as my mother always told me, "A watched pot never boils."

PERIODS OF SILENCE ARE ABOUT demonstrating your understanding and true trust in life. The farmer cannot make his crops grow any faster than the process will allow. By trying to force the crop to grow faster than it is ready to grow, he or she is likely to destroy it. Overwatering or overfertilizing does not work in favor of the desired result in this case but actually works against it. By accepting the divine timing of how life works and learning to cultivate from this truth, the farmer has the best chance of harvesting a hearty and abundant crop.

The surfer does not paddle out into the ocean and then demand that a huge wave show up that he or she can ride. The surfer works hard to paddle out, get him or herself positioned correctly, and then stays ready for when the "big one" comes. The surfer is at the mercy of the entire ocean and its readiness. In the meantime, there may be many smaller waves that the surfer thought might be the one. Nonetheless he or she rides each while hoping the next one will be the one they imagined when the day began. The control the surfer has is to be prepared, patient, and in position for the one they dream about riding. The rest is up to life.

Your creative intentions function in very much the same way. There is a divine order to the process that must be respected. Pushing against the greater truth has karmic consequences that result in more "time" to create what you desire. Like swimming upstream, it is draining, and all the effort is unlikely to get you very far. You do everything you can and then rest in the acceptance that when the time is "right," it will happen. In the meantime, you rely on gratitude, belief, and faith in the universe, which has brought you to this moment.

"Faith isn't faith until it's all you're holding on to."

—UNKNOWN

. . .

THE FOLLOWING IS A STORY from my own life that highlights
the importance of having faith, enduring silence, and waiting for
the right time. Keep in mind that this could apply to the timing of
anything you are looking to create for yourself.

MY PARENTS WERE MARRIED very young. My mother was
eighteen and my father was twenty. They had me when my mom
was only twenty, and by the time my mom was twenty-five and
my dad was twenty-seven they had two more children: my sister
two years after me and my brother three years after that. As it
often happens with those who marry and have children at a young
age, my parents struggled. They both were having trouble taking
care of and financially supporting the family, while also trying to
discover who they were as individuals. They experienced financial
pressures and personal issues that took a toll on the marriage.

Although on some level, they loved each other dearly, this was
not enough to overcome the challenges that life presented them
with. They had some very basic differences in personalities and
passions. As I grew into my early teens, their marital problems,
occasional separations, and ultimate divorce had a profound effect
on me.

FORTUNATELY, I NEVER GAVE UP on the idea of marriage or
family; rather, I realized how important it was to connect with
someone with the same level of maturity, values, interests, and

intentions that I had. Love and attraction were a must, but these other issues proved to be equally if not more important in building a fulfilling life with someone.

Starting around age twelve or thirteen, I imagined the woman I wanted to marry. I imagined every detail about her, from her personality to her looks to her passions. I pictured what it would be like to be married to someone like this, and I often wondered where she was and what she was doing at the very moment I was thinking about all of this.

The reasons why my parents' marriage seemed so tumultuous at times became so simple when I really looked at who they each were as individuals and how young they were. This realization ended up being a true gift. I understood by watching my parents' struggle what wasn't working with their marriage and that in turn gave me the belief in what would work for me. I realized that if I searched long and hard enough for all the qualities and conditions that truly mattered to me in a partner, it would give me the best opportunity to find a relationship that would last a lifetime.

THIS WAS A POWERFUL BELIEF, and it strengthened my desire, intention, and faith tenfold as it related to finding my soul mate. As I dated in my late teens and through my years in college, I subconsciously evaluated every girl I spent time with to see if they even remotely matched the very clear image I had in my head. Did they match mentally and physically? And most important, did they match the deeper, mature, and more profound connection I was looking to make? I was so intent on finding this woman that I looked for her in the face and personality of every woman I met or dated. After being in a few serious relationships in college and afterward, I eventually chose to spend many evenings alone, rather than continue to date someone with whom I knew I was not compatible. This resulted in many quiet nights.

SO HERE IS WHERE the story gets very interesting as it relates to intention, desire, and timing. One night during my sophomore year of college, I went over to hang out at a good friend's apartment. As I walked in, I saw that the girl he was dating and a friend of hers were over, hanging out and listening to music. I was immediately drawn to the girlfriend's friend. As happenstance would have it, I eventually asked her out, and about a week later, we went out on a dinner date. We had a great time, and I remember being drawn to her personality and level of maturity, as well as her looks. The date ended with a nice kiss good-bye, and everything seemed like it was right to continue this relationship to see where it would go, except for one thing—timing. Beth was twenty-three and already out of college. I was just twenty and in the throes of the college experience. Even though there was a connection between us on some level that we were both aware of, it was as if something was telling us that we weren't ready yet to take it any further. After that night, I did not see her again for almost four years.

A few years later, now out of college, in the working world, and still on my quest, I bumped into her at a popular restaurant. We exchanged numbers and started dating. Over the next few months, we fell deeper and deeper in love. We eventually married, and almost twenty years and two children later, we are still going strong. I still remember the exact moment, three or four months into the relationship with her, when it just hit me that she was the woman I wanted to marry. Now I don't mean hit me like a tap on the shoulder. I mean hit me like a lightning strike to the head. I realized in an instant that the girl I had been searching for since I was thirteen years old, the one I had imagined down to the most finite detail and waited much of my life to find, was the very girl I was dating and falling in love with. The truth washed over me in that moment in a blanket of knowingness so strong and so right I will never forget it.

What is amazing about this experience is how powerfully life delivers you your true intentions and desires. In this case, due to the very strong yearning we both had to find our significant other, the universe put us together through a million wonderful sequences of perfect coincidences. What is interesting is that it was four years too soon! We both wanted to meet the right person so badly for so long that life relented and we drew our first meeting in way ahead of its divine timing. It couldn't work yet. We both had many life lessons to learn before we reconnected, but we never wavered in our faith that we each would eventually find the right person. That is what allowed us both to be available when the time was right. **Because my strong intention and faith in finding her, as well as her intention and faith in finding me, never wavered, serendipity brought us together again four years later—this time for good.**

YOU MAY FEEL LIKE YOU already had your shot at a career, relationship, or purpose in life that didn't work out; yet as the story of how I journeyed to the vision I set as a young teenager shows, you never know what is around the next corner. There is a perfect reason why it did not work out the first time, the second time, or the third time. **The key if you really want to make it happen is to keep your intention, desire, and, most important, your belief focused on what IS possible for you. Life may shock you with what happens next.**

The energy that probably carries the most weight as it relates to what manifested for both of us is FAITH.

Faith provided the patience necessary for us to make clear, un-hurried choices for our lives.

Faith provided the strength for each of us to get through the times in life when we both wished we had that significant person to share life with.

Faith allowed us both the strength to endure the many moments of silence along the way.

Faith is an act of honor to the elegant and creative universe, and faith is THE KEY to mastering the concept of time. This applies to every situation in life. Remember, you always have a choice in how you see and react to your circumstance.

Here Are a Few Self-Reflective Questions to Ponder:

- What attitude or belief do you feel best serves you right now as it relates to your most desired intent?
- Does being resistant to what life is offering you or refusing to accept the circumstance you are in help you on your quest?
- Does being cynical or losing faith help you in any way toward what you want for your life now?

"Doubt is a pain too lonely to know that faith is his twin brother."

—KHALIL GIBRAN

THERE WERE CERTAINLY MANY TIMES in my life when I wished things were different—times when I couldn't make sense of what was happening in my world and why I was facing the circumstances in front of me. What is incredible now is that I see the perfection of each past event, why I went through them, and how they have all led me to this very moment.

There is a beautiful perfection in the way life takes you through the twists, turns, and occasional silences. Trusting these times of silence and trusting in the fact that you've done all you can do are the signs of a maturing soul. Knowing at times that your situation simply needs to be left alone is a big part of demonstrating ultimate faith. It is the evidence that you are mastering time by finding the peace that can only be found in trusting and understanding that something new will always emerge.

This process is like switching a radio station when you no longer like the music. In between frequencies, there is a period of static and silence. But if you stay focused on finding a better station, eventually, a new, more pleasurable sound will be found. In the process you may discover a whole new spectrum of channels that you never knew existed—all because you were willing to take a chance, leave the current channel, and live through the silence and static.

Patience is a big part of faith. Your patience may be tested many times on your journey. There may be instances when your timetable may not match up with the one life is presenting to you. This is when the real test starts. How much faith do you truly have in yourself and in the way the world works? Your state of mind will always provide the answer.

> "Genius is eternal patience."
>
> —Michelangelo

A Word on the Word *God*

The following story is one of my favorites, as it relates to the rich concept of faith. Essentially, this story is about trusting life at every turn. But first, I'd like to discuss a word that is used throughout the story. The word is *God*.

There is a specific reason why I did not use this word to any great degree in my first book, *I AM*, and have also not focused on the concept in this book either. The reason is that I believe the word *God* to be the most sacred and subjective word or concept in existence. It has different meaning to the religious person as well as to the atheist. It has a certain way of being interpreted by those who are spiritual as well as by those who see life from a scientific perspective. The word *God* carries a different understanding, meaning, and value for every person in existence. Using the word *God*, in many cases, can create confusion in the midst of an attempt to have a meaningful discussion, because of the many different ideas, definitions, and beliefs that are often associated with it.

Personally, I believe the concept to be beyond words or definition, and that this is why the mere utterance of the word can immediately invoke misunderstanding. I believe this is why people of certain ancient cultures and religions do not even speak the word but simply bend at the knee upon the thought. How do you express infinity when any attempted expression of it immediately negates it?

THE FOLLOWING QUOTE COMES the closest to expressing the notion of "God" from my perspective.

> "The one thing that a fish can never find is water, and the one thing that man can never find is God."
>
> —ERIC BUTTERWORTH

HAVING SAID ALL OF THIS, the following is a beautiful story expressing a magical principle of life. The story is presented using the word *God*. Again, I have great respect for your personal definition, whatever it may be, and I do not wish to impose on this; however, this story has such a powerful message that I wanted to include it here. If you'd prefer, you can substitute the word *life* for the word *God*, and the same point will be made.

The Fern and the Bamboo—Author Unknown

One day I quit my job, my relationship, and my spirituality. I wanted to quit my life. So I went into the woods and decided to have one last talk with God.

"God," I said, "can you give me one good reason not to quit?"

The answer surprised me. "Look around," God said. "Do you see the fern and the bamboo?"

"Yes," I replied.

"When I planted the fern and the bamboo seeds, I took very good care of them. I gave them light and I gave them water. The fern quickly grew from the earth. Its brilliant green covered the floor. Yet at the same time, nothing came from the bamboo seed. But I did not give up on the bamboo," said God.

"In the second year the fern grew more vibrant and plentiful. And again, nothing came from the bamboo seed. But I did not give up on the bamboo," God said.

"In year three, as the fern continued to grow, there was still nothing from the bamboo seed. But still I would not give up on the bamboo," God repeated.

"Once again, in the fourth year, there was nothing from the bamboo seed as the fern now covered the entire floor of the forest. However, I never once gave up on the bamboo," God said.

"Then in the fifth year, a tiny sprout emerged from the earth. Compared to the fern, it seemed small and insignificant. But just six months later, the bamboo grew and rose to over one hundred feet tall.

"The bamboo had spent these five years growing roots.

These roots made it strong and gave it what it needed to grow tall and survive.

"I would not give any of my creations a challenge it could not handle," God said to me. "Did you know that all this time that you have been struggling, you have actually been growing roots?

"I would not give up on the bamboo. I will never give up on you. Don't compare yourself to others. The bamboo had a different purpose than the fern. Yet they both make the forest beautiful. Your time will come. You will rise high," God exclaimed.

"How high will I rise?" I asked.

"How high will the bamboo rise?" God asked in return.

"As high as it can?" I questioned.

"Yes," God said. "So be faithful on your journey and rise as high as you can every day. It is your destiny."

LOVING THE JOURNEY

"There are two ways to live your life. One is as though nothing is a miracle. The other is as though everything is a miracle."

—ALBERT EINSTEIN

All of life is a choice. You have before you in this moment the never-ending opportunity to decide how you will respond to life and each event and challenge that comes your way. You cannot change what has happened in your life, but you can continually shape and affect what will be in your next moment. How you choose to do this is the continually changing arc of your fate and will determine so much of your destiny. Your continual response to life will also have an immeasurable effect on all those connected to you.

The route of resistance and time is one way to go through life. The other way is the way of acceptance, faith, and peace. Embracing the idea that you cannot fail on the journey and that your time is never truly "up" can change everything for you. Dedicating yourself to the true wisdom of this statement is something you must be really ready for.

> "You can't change the past, but you can ruin the present by worrying about the future."
>
> —UNKNOWN

TAKE A MOMENT TO LOOK around your world, and you will see that there is not a single thing in existence that escapes the process of reduction and dissolution. Everything is in the throes of a certain level of decay right now. Every piece of matter is on its own timetable, some of it much more resistant to the pressures of life than others. Some species of fish and turtles live to be close to two hundred years old. Some living trees have been determined to be between two thousand and five thousand years old. Some forms of rock and marble take hundreds of thousands of years to decompose in even the slightest measurable amount. And of course, humans currently average around eighty years of life. **So time in this sense really is the measure of matter's resistance to the infinite possibility from which it is formed.**

The main point is that this transformative process is a part of everything in existence. You cannot avoid this—only gracefully accept it as the truth. Through your acceptance of this, you will develop a new energy and state of mind that will improve your quality of life and make every day seem timeless and priceless.

This state of grace has been sought throughout the ages. A state of presence and fulfillment with all that you are experiencing allows you to be in the most powerful state of mind. **When none of your energy is being used to resist any truth about life, all of your energy is used in a positive way to draw in exactly what you want to fulfill your biggest intentions.** Your attention is fully absorbed and present in the miracle and wonder of whatever is in front of you in every moment. Life becomes a magical experience of flow.

> "The important thing to you is not how many years in your life, but how much life in your years!"
>
> —EDWARD STIEGLITZ

AN ANALOGY THAT really emphasizes the way we can choose to move through life and determine time is that of going down a large waterslide. If before you slide down, your mind is full of fear and your body is tight and rigid, you will fight your way down the entire slide—rubbing up against the sides, slowing yourself down, and really not enjoying the trip very much. It will end being a very uncomfortable ride where you end up plopping clumsily into the pool of water at the bottom. If you feel excitement about the ride and have faith in the overall experience, however, your mind will be relaxed. As your mind relaxes, your body will also relax more, and you will be in less resistance with the slide. As a result, the ride will get faster and smoother and you will effortlessly glide along. You will end up soaring off the end of the slide and making a perfect entry into the pool.

In so many ways, this is exactly what life is like. You are on the ride of life whether you like it or not. You can go kicking and screaming, resisting what is in front of you while time seems to drag on and life evolves around you, or you can choose to embrace this amazing gift and immediately start enjoying the ride and all of its endless creativity and astounding beauty in each moment.

THE BEAUTY OF LETTING GO, releasing yourself from your past and from any resistance or fear of your future, is that you liberate yourself from the pains and chains of time. Thinking now dissolved, you are free to be and to powerfully radiate and create from a place of only possibility and love. It is then that you realize that the only moment you have to change your life is this one,

Or this one . . .

Or this one . . .

Or this one . . .

YOUR WHOLE EXPERIENCE BECOMES one big exciting creative experience. **There is no longer such a thing as wasted time, because you have found the meaning in all of it.** Purpose and gratitude are found in the most mundane of situations, like standing in line, riding a bus, doing the laundry or dishes. A new appreciation is found for the endless moment of life. You find that true personal empowerment is realized by trusting life in every moment.

> When you reach the ultimate conclusion that life is here to serve you, the only thing left to decide is what you feel worthy of receiving.

THE LIGHT OF LOVE IS always shining on you. To feel it, you must trust that it is there even when you can't see it. You must understand that no matter what you are going through at this moment, this love *is* working with you so that you may persevere and come to an even greater and more liberating understanding of who and what you really are. *Fear not, for in each day and in every moment all is being revealed . . .*

CONTAINING THE
JOY AND LAUGHTER

*The only absolute truth is infinite possibility; everything else is a
function of time and relativity, the womb of your endless journey of
becoming this truth.*

So here you are now, forever in the middle of your endless journey of creation. You have read the material in this book for an
exact reason. You have drawn it in as a perfect part of an endless
stream of information to help you along your way. You may have
come to this material with the following questions: How can I
understand more about life? How do I change my experience?
How do I gain more control over my life? How do I actually create
what I desire? How do I master the experience of time? How do I
live life with a greater sense of peace and contentment?

Each of these questions has an answer. Many of these answers
have already been presented to you and are simply waiting for you
to decide when the "time" is right for you to embrace them. Many
future circumstances will present them as well. **(These answers
are your destiny.)**

Awakening to this reality is likely to produce uncontrollable laughter. Knowing that you cannot avoid your own edification and perfection can produce a state of surrender where laughter may be the only sane result. Each day then ends up being like a giant treasure hunt. What will life show me today? How will my questions and intentions be served? What ignorance will be revealed? How will time unfold next? It can be exciting to know that a new understanding of who you really are awaits you every single day!

Mastering Time Comes Down to Four Main Things:

1. A strong desire for new awareness
2. A love and belief in who you are that is without limits
3. A persistent demonstration of your intent
4. A faith and trust in every outcome

CREATING AT THE SPEED of light is the result of creating from a completely fearless state of mind. It is pure intention in action. It also requires that you will never impose on, manipulate, or attempt to control the free will of another human being as you move through the process. The great magic in the movement of creation comes from a deep and unconditional love and respect for life itself. It is this unspoken understanding that works to "move mountains" for you.

THERE MAY BE THE NUISANCE of recurring habits that seem to not want to go away easily. Do not be dismayed. The most effective thing you can do is to learn to honor and respect each moment for the sacred gift that it is for you. **You do this by avoiding the trap of feeling bad about yourself when you fall into an old habit**, by accepting the importance of where you are in the process, by finding love for who you are, regardless of circumstance, and by trusting that your true intention and desire will emerge.

I'LL NEVER FORGET the first time I was introduced to this concept. It was when I was around the age of fifteen and had just realized how challenging my family's financial situation was. I recognized that I would not be able to count on my parents to have enough money to send me to college. Money was very tight in our house and my parents were burdened with other more pressing financial responsibilities. My dream of going to college seemed like a remote possibility. Upon coming to this realization, I was visibly upset. My mother looked at me, immediately saw the tears, and asked me what was wrong. I explained that I was upset because I had no idea how, given the current financial situation, I was ever going to be able to afford to go to college.

It was then that my mother did something I have not forgotten to this day. Even though she was going through a tough time of her own and was often distracted, she had the incredible wisdom to get down on one knee, put her hands on my shoulders, look straight into my eyes, and in a tone that could only come from a mother's love, say, "Howie, when you strongly believe in something for yourself and put your heart and mind fully toward it, anything is possible for you. Never forget this."

Those incredibly wise and powerful words have been a part of everything I have envisioned and worked for in my life thus far, including going to and graduating from college. The idea of putting the mind to an intention and not being deterred by any challenges, struggles, and unforeseen circumstances along the way has played out over and over in my life. A strong belief and faith in what *is* possible is what has allowed these words to find their way to this very book. This power is a part of every aspect of my life and everyone I meet. It is part of every single aspect of yours as well.

If you knew how powerful you truly are, you would never stop smiling.

THIS MAGNIFICENT POWER IS ALWAYS yours to claim. It is the way we look at ourselves and our world that determines so much of what becomes our experience. Becoming aware of how you see the world and act within it is a huge step of awareness on the road to mastering the experience of time and life.

SOME YEARS AGO, I RECEIVED an e-mail from someone I counseled that is a perfect expression of this point. As he explained some of the things he learned about himself from our meeting, this wonderful gem was revealed:

"What I have learned is that my response is my responsibility. This demonstrates who I AM. One does not cause me to be the way I AM; one reveals the way I AM."

· · ·

THE TREASURE IN SEEING OURSELVES clearly is that we get to see more of what it is that keeps us from our hearts' desires. We come to understand why our desires had seemed far off in the future. We see what is creating our reality of TIME.

> **Mastery over life is not so much a discipline as it is an inten-tion, not so much in need of a strong energy as a strong belief, not necessarily hard to achieve but readily available to those with a deep desire, a pure heart, and a strong faith in life.**

THE "HOW" OF DOING THIS is found in the strength of your desires. You must be committed to the process of understanding yourself and life. Reading this or other material is an absolute con-firmation that you are fully engaged in this process. You are doing it right now.

Sometimes your actions will produce exactly what you desire, and sometimes they won't. But either way, the key is to learn from the experience and keep going, to never give up in the pursuit of your desires and dreams. After all, you have all of eternity to com-plete them!

The universe is here to support you in every way possible along the way by constantly reflecting back to you the difference between what you say you want to experience and who you demonstrate that you are. Let me say this again. **The universe is constantly show-ing you the difference between what you say that you want and who you demonstrate that you are.** When what you say that you want is aligned with who you are demonstrating yourself to be, time collapses.

Time will always be what you make of it.

YOU CANNOT FAIL. In order just to be here now, you have gone through many challenging times in your life. Even when you had no idea how you were going to get through these trying moments, you still made it. The real beauty is that you always will. This universe will constantly support you, as it is doing now with these words. The only thing that the universe cannot do is choose for you. Only you can choose who you desire to be in this world—you have to do this under your own terms and in your own time.

When you combine the desire to change who you are with a newfound faith, love, and understanding in who you can be, however, fear doesn't stand a chance of holding you back. You are truly open and free to experience the infinite possibilities of self-expression, and the incredible sense of love, peace, and fulfillment that comes with it, in every aspect of your life.

The question to ask yourself at the end of this book is "Who am I?" Remember, you cannot create the experience of anything you have not chosen to fully believe in. The key is in declaring a new you, believing in a new you, and demonstrating the belief by acting as a new you. You have the pen; the story is yours to write. What will you write for yourself today?

> "The least movement is of importance to all nature. The entire ocean is affected by a pebble."
>
> —BLAISE PASCAL

THERE IS NO ONE WHO is more powerful than you. In this moment, you have a golden opportunity to align with your heart's true desire. In this moment, you have the opportunity to honor your perfection by freely releasing more of the powerful, endless love that is inside you to everyone in your daily walk of life. This is the essence of how your world positively changes.

> "Every moment is the right moment."
>
> —SATHYA SAI BABA

HERE IS A STORY HIGHLIGHTING the opportunity that is always in front of you:

One night, as he walked past the home of a shoemaker, Rabbi Salanter noticed that despite the late hour, the shoemaker was still working by the light of a dying candle. "Why are you still working?" he asked the man.

"It is very late and soon that candle will go out," the shoemaker replied. "As long as the candle is still burning, it is still possible to accomplish and to mend."

Rabbi Salanter spent that entire night excitedly pacing his room and repeating to himself: "As long as the candle is still burning, it is still possible to accomplish and to mend, as long as the candle is still burning, it is still possible to accomplish and to mend."

No matter what has happened in your life up to this point, the same opportunity exists for you to accept that life knows better than you the reasons why you are where you are. You have the golden opportunity to start from this precious moment anew—all the while knowing you cannot run out of time and you cannot fail. Could there be anything more exciting than knowing that there is an eternal moment of unlimited possibility in front of you? Could it be any more hopeful to know that this moment is the moment in which it can all begin to change?

> "Don't write your name on sand, waves will wash it away.
> Don't write your name on the sky, winds will blow it away.
> Write your name in the hearts of people you come in touch with, that is where it will stay."
>
> —Unknown

.   .   .

THE GREATEST GIFT YOU CAN give your world is an open hand
and a loving heart that stem from a loving self and an acceptance
of all of life. This comes from a deep knowing that you are truly
worth it all. It is through this knowledge that the power in you
shines like the brightest star and impacts your world in the most
healing and loving way possible. Mastering life and time begins
and ends with mastering yourself. By the simple act of intending
to master your mind and heart you release a powerful gift to all of
mankind. Your ultimate offering to the world is the result of your
own self-understanding and self-love.

There is nothing as important as the way you decide to interpret and respond to life. Responding from a place of the highest
faith and love is how you enrich the moments of your life and direct the creative energy around you. **You are the creator of time.
You are the ultimate guru of the journey. You are the master of
your reality. Life and all of time are endlessly beholden to you!**

Forever

All I've ever been
All I've ever seen
All I've ever known
Life
A journey of pain and laughter
Days of sorrow and joy
There is no escape but acceptance
There is no answer but now
There is no reason but these words
How beautifully simple
To be in this space
To embrace this moment
To feel this love
Thus ending time
Forever.

ACKNOWLEDGMENTS

There are so many who contributed in one way or another to the journey I have been on that has produced this book and its contents. I am grateful for each and every one of you.

More specific, I'd like to thank Sara Carder for her continued faith in my work; Joanna Ng for her wonderful editorial help; Brianna Yamashita for her marketing expertise; Amy Hughes for her continued guidance and support; Stephanie Gunning for her trusted professional eye; and Jen Rogers and Lori Jung for their professionalism, enthusiasm, friendship, and deep conviction in my path and the work.

To my moral support team, whose faith and love is unwavering I am in the deepest gratitude: Tracy, Gary, Mom, Dad, Donna, Claude, Kenny, Tarasa, Eli, and Michael.

To my two greatest gifts, Sydney and Jeffrey, you inspire me and make me proud every day. And, to my soul mate, Beth, your unwavering faith, wisdom, conviction, support, and love is such an immeasurable part of this work. My gratitude and love for it and for you transcends all of time.

And lastly, to you, the reader of these words. Thank you for allowing this material to be a part of your life's path. May your continual experience of life be known only from a place of the highest beauty, peace, love, and eternal joy.

ABOUT THE AUTHOR

Howard Falco is a self-empowerment expert and modern-day spiritual teacher and speaker on the nature of consciousness, reality, and the power of the mind. His first book was *I AM: The Power of Discovering Who You Really Are* (Tarcher/Penguin, September 2010).

In 2002, at age thirty-five, Howard experienced a sudden and massive expansion of awareness that left him with a clear understanding of the creative power of all of life and the origins of all human action and inaction, joy, and suffering. He has since set out to honor his experience and insight by sharing all that he discovered.

Through his work he guides everyone, from professional athletes to business executives, to new, liberating insights and self-awareness as it relates to removing fear, breaking through limits, and achieving a new level of peace in life. The intention is to offer each individual a more powerfully creative state of mind that leads to a new and more desired personal reality.

His biggest message is that regardless of the current circumstance we find ourselves in, we all have the same access to the understanding and wisdom that answers our deepest questions and brings true inner peace. We only have to realize that each of us are both capable and worthy of experiencing it.

Howard grew up in Chicago, graduated from Arizona State University, and now lives in Arizona with his wife and two children. More information about his speaking, private coaching work, and schedule can be found at www.howardfalco.com.